Ethics without God?

Classici della filosofia contemporanea

Regione Siciliana
Assessorato ai Beni Culturali ed Ambientali ed alla Pubblica Istruzione

Other Titles of Interest from St. Augustine's Press and Dumb Ox Books
Aristotle, *Aristotle – On Poetics*
Aristotle, *Physics, Or Natural Hearing*
Plato, *The Symposium of Plato: The Shelley Translation*
St. Augustine, *On Order [De Ordine]*
St. Augustine, *The St. Augustine LifeGuide™*
Thomas Aquinas, *Commentary on the Epistle to the Hebrews*
Thomas Aquinas, *Commentaries on St. Paul's Epistles to Timothy, Titus, & Philemon*
Thomas Aquinas, *Commentary on Aristotle's Nicomachean Ethics*
Thomas Aquinas, *Commentary on Aristotle's De Anima*
Thomas Aquinas, *Commentary on Aristotle's Metaphysics*
Thomas Aquinas, *Commentary on Aristotle's Posterior Analytics*
Thomas Aquinas, *Commentary on Aristotle's Physics*
Thomas Aquinas, *Disputed Questions on Virtue*
Henry of Ghent, *Henry of Ghent's* Summa of Ordinary Questions: *Article One: On the Possibility of Human Knowledge*
John of St. Thomas, *Introduction to the Summa Theologiae of Thomas Aquinas*
John Poinsot, *Tractatus de Signis*
Francisco Suarez, *On Creation, Conservation, & Concurrence*
Francisco Suarez, *Metaphysical Demonstration of the Existence of God*
John Paul II, *The John Paul II LifeGuide™*
Josef Pieper and Heinz Raskop, *What Catholics Believe*
Josef Pieper, *Scholasticism: Personalities and Problems*
Josef Pieper, *The Silence of St. Thomas*
Josef Pieper, *The Concept of Sin*
Josef Pieper, *Death and Immortality*
C.S. Lewis, *The Latin Letters of C.S. Lewis*
Jacques Maritain, *Natural Law*
Yves R. Simon, *The Great Dialogue of Nature and Space*
Gabriel Marcel, *The Mystery of Being* (in two volumes)
Gabriel Marcel, *Man against Mass Society*
Gabriel Marcel, *Thou Shall Not Die*
Dietrich von Hildebrand, *The Heart: An Analysis of Human and Divine Affectivity*
Dietrich von Hildebrand, *The Dietrich von Hildebrand LifeGuide™*
Richard Peddicord, O.P., *The Sacred Monster of Thomism: An Introduction to the Life and Legacy of Reginald Garrigou-Lagrange, O.P*
Florent Gaboriau, *The Conversion of Edith Stein*. Translated by Ralph McInerny.
Charles Cardinal Journet, *The Mass: The Presence of the Sacrifice of the Cross*
Ralph McInerny, *The Defamation of Pius XII*
Ralph McInerny, *Some Catholic Writers*
Ralph McInerny, *Let's Read Latin* (with audio CD)
James V. Schall, S.J., *The Sum Total of Human Happiness*
James V. Schall, S.J., *The Regensburg Lecture*
Peter Kreeft, *The Philosophy of Jesus*
Peter Kreeft, *Jesus-Shock*
Servais Pinckaers, O.P., *Morality: The Catholic View*

Ethics without God?

The Divine in Contemporary Moral and Political Thought

Edited by
Fulvio Di Blasi, Joshua P. Hochschild, and Jeffrey Langan

ST. AUGUSTINE'S PRESS
South Bend, Indiana
2008

In association with

Thomas International

Manufactured in the United States of America.

1 2 3 4 5 6   14 13 12 11 10 09 08

Library of Congress Cataloging in Publication Data
Ethics without God?: the divine in contemporary moral and political thought /
edited by Fulvio Di Blasi, Joshua P. Hochschild, and Jeffrey Langan.
p. cm.
Includes bibliographical references.
ISBN-13: 978-1-58731-225-0 (paperbound: alk. paper)
ISBN-10: 1-58731-225-5 (paperbound: alk. paper)
1. Ethics. 2. Religious ethics. 3. Religion and politics. I. Di Blasi, Fulvio.
II. Hochschild, Joshua P., 1972– III. Langan, Jeffrey, 1970–
BJ37.E797 2007
170.9 – dc22   2007030832

∞ The paper used in this publication meets the minimum requirements of the
American National Standard for Information Sciences – Permanence of Paper
for Printed Materials, ANSI Z39.48–1984.

ST. AUGUSTINE'S PRESS
www.staugustine.net

TABLE OF CONTENTS

PREFACE

Philosophy, at least the philosophy of the fourth century B.C., the golden age of Greek philosophy, begins in crisis. Socrates, Plato and Aristotle are all, in their different ways, carrying on a continuing argument with sophistry. Plato's *Protagoras* presents a Socrates confronting the seductive suggestion that what is true for you is true for you, and what is true for me is true for me. So too when Aristotle dwells at such length on the principle of contradiction in Book Four of the *Metaphysics*, he sees the denial of this principle as dispiriting to the young. It will not do to treat the sophistic position as one option among others, or suggest that in this matter we can simply agree to disagree. To do that would be to treat acceptance of the principle of contradiction as something some people choose and others reject. And then we would not have alternatives: both positions would be merely subjective.

That is why the denial of the first principle or the relativizing of moral judgments must be shown to be, not a tenable position, but one which undermines itself and lands its holder in deep incoherence. Relativism is simply not an option, and this must be shown in terms of what the relativist implicitly appeals to.

Such efforts merely clear the ground and have, as Aristotle suggested, the effect of inspiriting the beginner with the conviction that sophistry is not an intelligible option. Then more positive inquiry can begin.

Such contributions as those of Alasdair MacIntyre and now John Rist, prompted as they both are by the realization that something has gone radically wrong in modernity, must begin with some version of the task that Plato and Aristotle set themselves against sophistry. In their different ways, MacIntyre and Rist recognize that philosophy is in crisis and can only be rehabilitated by prolonged discussion of the positions that have undermined it. In many ways they are fighting their way back to the starting points, to ineluctable principles.

It is the crisis in moral philosophy that takes pride of place in these efforts. The crisis in epistemology is always in the wings, but first things first. Is moral decision grounded in the way things are, or is it something that must be seen as the working out of one or another position arbitrarily chosen? Are moral agents isolated instances of freedom or do human beings share common principles without which personal and communal life is impossible? Russ Hittinger has shown that any effort to interpret the moral thought of Thomas Aquinas as if the fact/value dichotomy were the unavoidable *laissez-passer* is to flirt with the flaws of modernity.

Part of the crisis of modern philosophy has been the balkanization of the disciplines. Not only were there the many attempts to see philosophy and science as parallel tracks, but within philosophy itself, specialization led to the "doing" of moral philosophy in isolation from the other disciplines. Of course, in many cases, this was not merely an oversight, but an outright rejection of the relevance of other disciplines for doing ethics.

The guiding question of the essays in this volume is: Can moral philosophy be developed without reference to God? That question leads to the realization that until and unless moral philosophy is seen as one of a number of disciplines making up philosophy it will fall short of its aims. There is no way that the human agent can be adequately understood apart from the natural world of which he is a part, related to other physical beings with whom he shares many traits. And there is no way in which moral philosophy can be adequately considered if it is wrenched from its place in a *paideia* defined as the love of wisdom, with wisdom in turn defined as such knowledge of the divine as man can achieve.

It is the successful achievement of that preliminary work that has permitted so-called virtue ethics to arise. Virtue ethics has little in common with medieval studies or other efforts to reoccupy the past. Nonetheless, seeing the continuing relevance of the moral thought of antiquity and the Middle Ages is a mark of Virtue Ethics. It is not the pastness of the past that interests it, but *ut ita dicam* the presence of the past.

Ralph McInerny
University of Notre Dame

INTRODUCTION

The classical distinction between philosophy and theology is often misunderstood. It is assumed that if theology is concerned with God, then philosophy must prescind from the notion of divinity. Thus, by further confusion, in the contemporary interpretation theology is "religious," and philosophy is by contrast "secular." When this interpretation, questionable enough on purely theoretical grounds, is read anachronistically back into the history of philosophy, the very beginning of philosophy in Greece is sometimes described as a turn away from the theological, a refusal to countenance the supernatural, and an attempt to explain everything by reference to natural causes.

In fact, however, while the first philosophers may have wanted to explain everything by the illumination of natural reason, they were not averse to supernatural or divine beings as objects of explanation and contemplation. Plato reports that Socrates responded to the charge of atheism by insisting that he had a higher, more pious view of divinity than his fellow citizens. Aristotle's major practical and theoretical works – the *Ethics* and the *Metaphysics* – each culminate in reflection on a god and the possibility of human beings grasping or participating in its divine activity. Rather than a turn away from the divine, Greek philosophy should be seen as an attempt to purify how man conceives of the divine. Greek philosophy was essentially theological.

The distinction between this kind of theology – "philosophical theology" or "natural theology" – and the theology appropriate for a particular religious faith – "revealed theology" or "sacred doctrine" – remained apparent through the medieval and early modern periods. So even when moral theory and political philosophy were considered in separation from religious faith, they could still be understood as having a theological dimension – that is, God may still play a role in accounting for the moral status of human acts, for the authority of rulers, for nature of the common good.

But it was not long before the secularization that isolated faith and reason from each other also isolated reason from any consideration of the divine. This would have particular consequences for moral thought. Nietzsche would eventually insist that traditional morality could not be sustained without God, but the project of modern philosophy largely assured that morality did not depend, metaphysically or epistemologically, on theological commitment. Indeed, as Nietzsche saw, the development of modern philosophy and human-rights politics was closely connected to the famous Grotian hypothesis *etiamsi dare-mus non esse Deum* – ethics, it was claimed, could be grounded on nature considered as something wholly independent of God; moral philosophy could proceed apace even if we ventured to suppose that God did not exist.

Alas, this venture proved far from benign. Not long after the role of God was displaced, the very idea of nature itself was strongly challenged too, and skepticism, nihilism, and the will to power combined, in the 19th and 20th centuries, with the strongest movements of practical and theoretical atheism ever seen in human history. The moral cost of this theoretical experiment is beyond accounting. It is a welcome turn of events that recent generations of scholars have sought to inform their perspective on the modern condition through a retrieval of pre-modern thought, especially its attention to metaphysical and theological frameworks.

The essays in this volume attempt to bring a theological perspective to bear on a variety of current political and theoretical questions. The main essays explore a place for the role of God in ethical and political thought. Jeffrey Langan explores the persistence of God in American political documents and political philosophy, and considers how a striving after the divine might play a role in political education. James Kreuger offers a sympathetic, and implicitly Thomistic, reading of Kant: If Kant's ethics is not to slip into consequentialism (as it does in some interpretations), we must interpret Kant as ultimately uniting happiness (the good we seek) with morality (right action) by making the latter causally constitutive of the former – something only possible given the assumption of the immortality of the soul and the existence of God.

Laura Garcia challenges various attempts to justify substantive moral claims within a materialistic (and so atheistic) framework. Genuine ethics, as she argues, must be grounded on a more robust metaphysics. The notion of natural law rests on a more sophisticated conception of nature than materialism offers – a conception available to reason, but into which faith provides powerful insight.

David Thunder takes up a central question in contemporary political philosophy – the nature of deliberative democracy, and particularly the role of religious discussion in public discourse. Reviewing some of the well-known difficulties of a liberal "principle of restraint" which excludes religious discourse, Thunder considers the advantages of regulating discourse with reference to virtues governing the behavior of communication rather than rules governing speech content. Virtues of communication would not necessarily rule out religious interventions in public discourse – the appropriateness and effectiveness of such interventions would have to be judged by the prudence of virtuous citizens.

The volume also offers extended explorations of two recent books, each of which represents a major scholarly venture in theologically realist ethical thought. In 2002, John Rist published a vigorous defense of Platonism against various historical alternatives in moral philosophy. His book *Real Ethics* (Cambridge, 2002) provides an occasion for reflection and friendly critical engagement by four scholars – a theologian, two philosophers, and a media the̅orist. Likewise, Russell Hittinger's *The First Grace* (ISI Books, 2003) offers penetrating analysis of Thomistic natural law in moral philosophy, political theory, and jurisprudence. Here his book elicits a variety of reflections from relevant disciplines. Each set of essays is followed by a generous response from the featured author himself.

God, Nietzsche and Contemporary Political Philosophy

Jeff Langan

Introduction

How does God figure in contemporary political philosophy in the United States? If we consult authorities in the field, the answer we may expect is, "not much." Have scholars lost a sense of wonder about man, the world, and God? It is true that many contemporary political theorists tend to focus narrowly on debates about the nature, function, and dangers of democracy. However, we can find a few strands of contemporary political philosophy that exhibit willingness to discuss the role of God in political philosophy, and even see the question as having central importance.

Ever since Nietzsche's proclamation in the nineteenth century that "God is dead," at least one segment of political philosophy has attempted to understand this position and deal with its consequences. (Nietzsche also thought that once this proposition made its way into political and social life, it would lead to violent ideological conflict.[1]) At least three schools of thought on the contemporary scene in the United States have attempted to address the consequences of Nietzsche's claim: the Thomists, the Straussians (Leo Strauss and his students), and the Voegelinians (Eric Voegelin and his students).[2] Rather than take Nietzsche's claim as an invitation to ignore God, their responses have shown that the problem of God and political philosophy is important to the continuing study of politics, that it relates to practical questions (how to organize a political

---

1 Catherine Zuckert, *Postmodern Platos*, University of Chicago Press, 1995, p. 88.
2 Leo Strauss and Eric Voegelin were both German immigrants to the United States. They both attempted to understand and meet the challenge of modern German philosophy. Both of them, with different results, saw a return to the ancients as a starting point for confronting the modern challenge (See also *Fides et Ratio* no. 85). At one point in the 1950's the two carried on an extended correspondence, one of the central themes being the role of faith and reason in political philosophy and the importance of God for political thought. This correspondence was published in *Faith and Political Philosophy*, ed. by Peter Emberly and Barry Cooper, 1993.

community that respects and responds to the fact of religious belief), and more philosophical questions (how religious belief helps or hinders the pursuit of wisdom).

In studying the problem as it exists in the context of American public life, the Voegelinians have emphasized that, in many ways, God is very much present and part of American political life and political philosophy. As a starting point, they would point to the signs of God's existence that regularly show themselves in American political and public life.[3]

A Voegelinian could not help but follow with some interest the debates taking place in Europe over whether to include a reference to God in the European Constitution. From this side of the Atlantic, an observer might ask, what is the ruckus about? At least in popular society and in the political culture of the United States, references to the name of God are not uncommon. *Time* magazine recently had a large portion of an issue dedicated to the faith of the current president. On July 8th, 2003, in an address delivered in Senegal on the topic of slavery, the president stated: "All the generations of oppression under the laws of man could not crush the hope of freedom and defeat the purpose of God . . . Enslaved Africans heard the ringing promises of the Declaration of Independence and asked the self-evident question, then why not me?" Later in his speech, still echoing the Declaration, he asserts: "the rights of African Americans were not the gift of those in authority. Those rights were granted by the Author of Life and regained by the persistence and courage of African Americans themselves."[4] The idea lurking behind the president's statement is that somehow, God as he is recognized in the Declaration, has a place in American politics. The president still includes a reference to God in the oath that he makes before taking office.

One could contrast this with an event that shocked Canadians in the Spring 2002. A potential candidate for prime minister mentioned God in one of his speeches. This caused quite a stir, as no public figure with aspirations for the post of prime minister had done such a thing in over a decade.[5] In the United States, presidents regularly make references to God in their speeches.

Back to the United States, Congress still has a chaplain. "In God We Trust" appears on our money. At least 80% of Americans still profess a belief in God.[6] An anonymous person or group has rented space on many billboards throughout the country placing messages from God in white letters in a black background. None of these examples are meant to prove much, other than the fact

3   Ellis Sandoz, *Republicanism, Religion, and the Soul of America*, University of
    Missouri Press, 2006; *A Government of Law: Political Theory, Religion, and the
    American Founding*, University of Missouri Press, 2001.
4   *New York Times,* July 9th 2003, section A, page 8; *Boston Globe*, July 9th 2003, A1.
5   "Is Day Using God for Gain?" *Chatham Daily News*, March 6, 2002.
6   Gallup Poll, May 2003.

that God appears in our political and social life. A Voegelinian would take this as a starting point to argue that an openness to some transcendent being is necessary for a healthy political order. And so, it is good that reminders of his existence are found in many places. This is a cause of concern to some. To others it is a breath of fresh air.

The purpose of this paper is not to evaluate the status of religious belief in the United States, nor is it to give an account of civil religion, per se, in the United States. Instead, it is to examine whether there is a political philosophy that grounds these popular expressions and to what extent is that political philosophy open to the conclusions of natural theology. I believe that there is such a political philosophy, and that and that it can fruitfully engage the resources of the American tradition.

At least one of America's founding documents, *The Declaration of Independence*, articulates a natural theology, and its meaning is still central to debates about the meaning of American Democracy. The natural theology of the *Declaration* might not be particularly robust, but its references to God are the result of the philosophical and practical reflection of the founding fathers on politics. The statements that they made offer at least an initial proposal of what people of different faiths and perhaps even philosophers could agree about God, using the light of their reason. It is also a starting point for avoiding some of the ills that could be associated with a society that makes no references to a divine source and standard of justice in thinking about itself, its citizens, and its role in the world. Of course theological invocation can be abused, or inconsistently integrated with practical life – Allan Wolfe notes that many American Christians profess a belief in God, yet quite easily take up the modes of behavior associated with new age spirituality. But the theological references in the *Declaration* provide a framework within which we can think about ourselves, our society, the world, and how we relate to them.

The *Declaration* makes four mentions of God, which together refer to God in three ways: as the God of nature, as God the Creator, and as the God of Providence. The first reference is to God as the God of nature. The signers of the *Declaration* argue that it is necessary to dissolve their political bonds with England and to assume "the separate and equal station to which the laws of nature and of nature's God entitle them." Next, they refer to God as the Creator, who has created men with rights. They assert that "all men are created equal," and that they "are endowed by their Creator with certain inalienable rights." Finally, they refer to the God of Providence. After listing their grievances and their reasons for separating from England, they appeal to the "Supreme Judge of the world for the rectitude of [their] intention," and state their "firm reliance on the protection of Divine Providence."

I do not think that it is overly controversial to suggest that the political philosophy, and perhaps the natural theology as well, underlying the *Declaration* is mostly that of John Locke's. Thomas Jefferson, the principal author of the document, is well-known for his Lockean tendencies, as are many of the American founders. At the same time, it seems that the third and fourth references to God were not written by Jefferson. They were later added by the Continental Congress.[7]

By and large, a Christian strand of Lockean political philosophy guided the first developments in American political history and thought. However, perhaps beginning in the late-nineteenth century and certainly by the end of the millennium, the Lockean synthesis came under scrutiny. Some challenges came as the result of attempts to re-cast American liberalism in Hegelian, pragmatic, utilitarian, or Kantian terms, or some combination thereof. Many of these attempts, unwittingly or not, and some for different reasons than others, have left God out of the picture of political philosophy. They have done so because in part their overall approach to philosophy involved developing political theories that leave out not only natural theology, but also metaphysics and other branches of philosophy that deal with immaterial substances and final causality. Others confuse metaphysics or natural theology as being the same thing as religious belief or faith. Some have the tendency towards an unhealthy secularism that goes far beyond that envisioned by the founding fathers and so they become overly sensitive when seeing references to God as part of a political philosophy, thinking that this implies an outright necessity to accept Christian belief.

Challengers to the Nineteenth Century synthesis have also arisen from outside of the ranks of the liberals. Some Christians would rather see God completely left out of political philosophy. They believe their faith to be irrational and any philosophy that would try to prove God's existence using reason would be foolish. Perhaps the biggest challenge in academic circles (at least in numbers) has come from the post-modernists. Post-modernists tend to side with the secularists in wanting to keep religious belief, metaphysics, and God out of public discourse. Many have a bone to pick with those who use reason as well. Having said that, there is an anti-secularist camp developing within the ranks of the secularists. This camp criticizes secularist liberals for being too fanatical, too religious, in their attempts to exclude God from public and philosophic discourse.[8] What I would like to do in this part of the paper is to show what stance a post-modern anti-secularist might take towards God, as He is referred to in the *Declaration*.

---

7   Michael Zuckert, *The Natural Rights Republic: Studies in the Foundation of the American Political Tradition*, University of Notre Dame Press, 1996; *Protestantism and the American Founding*, ed. by Thomas Engeman and Michael Zuckert, University of Notre Dame Press, 2004.

8   William Connolly, *Pluralism*, Duke University Press, 2005; *Powers of the Secular Modern*, edited by David Scott and Charles Hirshkind.

Engaging the Declaration

A recent book, *Why I am Not a Secularist* made a mini-splash among students of politics a few years back. In that and other works, its author claims to follow the tradition of thought founded by Lucretius and continued in modern times by the likes of Spinoza and Nietzsche,[9] calling it "immanent naturalism." The immanent naturalist would see at least two seemingly contradictory strands in the Declaration. On the one hand, the Declaration gives a pre-eminent place in institution-building, social control, and law-making to those who hold some form of theism. Theists have a tendency to fanaticism in holding to and promoting their position, to the point of excluding other modes of seeing morality. On the other hand, the *Declaration* allows for secular rights theories. The holders of these rights theories also have fanatical tendencies that lead them to exclude theists or believers on other modes of understanding the universe. The immanent naturalist seeks to engage these theorists so as to allow for more diverse modes of belief in a society, preventing the predominance or triumph of any one way of thinking about morality and politics.[10]

Now, I would like to look at the immanent naturalist position in more detail. When looking at the references to God in the *Declaration of Independence*, a nontheist would probably make the following points. Clearly, the *Declaration* does not support one Christian faith. Nevertheless, religious faith has had and continues to have a tremendous influence on society and politics. By referring to God, the *Declaration* puts forth God as the sign or standard of moral virtue and the condition of legitimate participation in national politics.[11] Two problems result: the *Declaration* supports religious faith over nonreligious faith, and the *Declaration* uses either religious faith or an understanding of rationalistic rights as an aid in nation-building.

Finding fault with an aspect of the *Declaration* its signers were proud of, the immanent naturalist asserts that taking seriously the references to God in the *Declaration* can render a number of people suspect without enforcing any particular version of Christianity. The founders thought that by referring to the God of nature, they were referring to an understanding of God that all persons could come to using their reason and independent of what their faith might tell them about God. But the references to God in the Declaration ask too much. Most citizens in such a country will opt for a morality that is based on the supersensible realm, and it will put theistic philosophers such as Taylor, Levinas, Ricoeur, MacIntyre, and Sandel at an advantage in debates about the existence of God

---

9   Connolly, *Neuropolitics: Thinking, Culture, Speed*, University of Minnnesota Press, 2002, pp. 75–76.

10   Ibid., p. 105.

11   Connolly, *Why I am Not A Secularist*, University of Minnesota Press, 1999, p. 109–110.

and the effects that a proof for the existence of God might have on how we think about human nature, society, law and justice.

In addition to giving theists an unfair advantage in public and academic debates, the *Declaration* uses its religious or supersensible qualities (rights) to foster nation-building. The God of the *Declaration* is the God of equality and rights, who exercises a providential care for a particular people. This idea of God allows for the emergence of democratic prophets who will build a great nation or who will seek to recover a lost nation if they think it has been harmed or weakened.[12] These prophets might use the ideas contained in the Declaration to create institutions and rules governing whether and how people can participate in those institutions.[13] From this standpoint, rulers or the culture at large will develop humanly-constructed rules so as to exclude individuals who did not accept the dominant construction.

While this position sees a potential bias in the *Declaration* against non-Christians, it also sees signs of progress. Over the past century, atheists, agnostics, and secularists have made it possible for many models of morality to have an influence on public life. However, atheists, agnostics, and secularists tend to be just as exclusive and just as intolerant as their religious counterparts. In a situation where both the religious people and the secular people have a tendency to fanaticism, an unhealthy split will develop in society between theism and atheism with each side trying to keep out all competitors that do not conform to its vision of morality and politics.

Immanent naturalism does not want to argue whether or not God exists, at least as it is argued in the current paradigm of theism vs. atheism.[14] It sees an unhealthy religious fanaticism developing among rationalists and secularists that leads them to intolerance towards anybody, religious or non-religious, who might make a claim in public life that does not meet the secularist standard of rationality. In the same way, theists have a tendency towards intolerance towards anybody who does not uphold their religious belief. Rather than let himself be trapped in the paradigm of theism, atheism, or agnosticism, Connolly proposes nontheism. The paradigm of theism versus atheism prevents true critical thinking, refinement, creativity and independent re-thinking of social and political problems. For a secularist to try to contain those who believe in God would be erroneous, just as erroneous as the attempts by theists to exclude atheists from public positions.[15] A better position would be to engage the theist and the atheist position in a reflective way.[16]

---

12   Ibid., p. 112–13.
13   Ibid., p. 153–54.
14   The title of a recent book putting forth a debate between John Haldane and J.J. Smart, *Atheism and Theism*, Blackwell Publishers, 2003.
15   He recalls the difficulties of Bertrand Russell obtaining a position at CUNY in the 1950's.
16   Connolly, *Why I am Not A Secularist*, 1999, p. 2–5.

The task of a modern immanent naturalist is to keep up the agonistic contact in the hopes of developing an alternative spirituality to the nation-building spirituality fostered by the theories that come from the *Declaration*. The goal of this spirituality is to create a democratic ethos from a creative coalition from diverse places, to create a dense multidimensional pluralism with numerous constituencies: ethnic, gender, sexual, religious, metaphysical faiths, with no constituency making a claim for the center of the coalition.[17]

This conception of politics requires that those engaged in it resist attempts to define politics in terms of nature or of culture. Conceptions of culture, identity, ethics, even correspondence theories of truth contain within them some theological notions. They belie a structure that can be known. Underneath any assertion of a structure that can be known lies an assertion that there is a God who creates that structure. Connolly hopes to challenge, without rejecting, this position. He argues that a nontheist lacks the position above the field to make a judgment one way or the other.[18] His goal will be to show the paradoxes inherent in these positions so that he can engage them with his own paradoxes.[19]

Techniques, not Rules, of Engagement

Since the immanent naturalist rejects nation building and politics on a great scale, he proposes a micropolitical approach for challenging the theism vs. atheism paradigm. Since the supersensible realm is a dangerous fiction, whether it comes in the form of God or abstract rights, the immanent naturalist want to question whether we should conceive of a morality tied to the idea of a law or a Being that is located above the sensible realm.[20]

Since national politics is a construct or a fiction, the goal of the nonsecular nontheist is to develop techniques to be used in personal settings that expose and challenge rival traditions. The term to sum up these techniques is micropolitics. A theory of micropolitics teaches citizens to "work by artful means to magnify, enrich, or modify elements in an affective register not reachable by argument or conscious regulation alone."[21] It is close to what in the bad old days was called character formation, but it is character formation without an emphasis on doctrine.[22] When engaging on the level of the micropolitical, the political actor focuses on nature and the body rather than God and the soul.[23] The point is to develop techniques, even to run little nontheistic experiments on oneself and others, in order to convert the body to nontheism. These techniques include

---

17 Ibid., p. 112–13.
18 Connolly, *Neuropolitics,* 2002, p. 49.
19 Ibid., 26–28; Connolly, *Why I am Not A Secularist*, 1999, 15–16.
20 Connolly, *Why I am Not A Secularist*, 1999, p. 169–70.
21 Connolly, *Neuropolitics*, 2002, p. 28.
22 Connolly, *Why I Am Not A Secularist,* 1999, pp. 26–27.
23 Connolly, *Neuropolitics*, 2002, pp. 84–85.

words, gestures, images, sounds, rythms, smells, and touches that define perception, thinking, identity, belief, and judgments. They can be applied in family, Church, school, military, talk shows, dramas, work, neighborhood gangs, sports events, charitable organizations, advertising, courtrooms, and police routines.[24] In each of these social relations, our actions say something about our intellectual and religious attachments. Therefore, immanent naturalists should work on techniques of the body for changing the intellectual and religious attachments of people in all of these situations.

Being Engaged

The techniques of the body are meant to offer a practical way for engaging political actors who might act as if the constructs of the Declaration are true. The purpose of such techniques is to help develop in all citizens a gratitude towards the openness of being. The secularist and the theist constructs have a tendency to prevent true gratitude towards being. The theist sees God as a source of morality and justice. The other, more secular, strand of thought sees in the *Declaration* a theory of rights or laws of nature above the sensible realm. The few who have insight into these laws would be able to take a stance of superiority towards those who either believe in God or towards immanent naturalists. The immanent naturalist hopes that an attachment to life and to the world and an openness to the possibility of being will develop generosity, forbearance, and responsibility.[25] He does this by not committing to the atheist or the theist position, but by touching them without articulating them.[26] He remains open to the quest for wholeness. He leaves open the possibility of converting to theism without insisting on his version of nontheism. He allows for currents of other traditions to influence his gratitude for being without reducing himself to the other traditions.[27]

The immanent naturalist sees that nontheism is a dangerous game. He sees that it can lead to a cynical view of the person and the world. Nontheism tends in the direction of apathy, and indifference to the point of creating a complete passivity towards being and life. There is no guarantee that the nontheistic gratitude to the rich abundance of being will continue in the face of injury, loss, violence or brutality. There is also no guarantee that nontheism puts the person at a greater risk of committing evil. It can easily lead to ideological manipulation or to further alienation.[28] One might add, in a world where nontheists cannot

---

24   Ibid., pp. 18–20, 75–76.
25   Connolly, *Neuropolitics,* 2002, pp. 85–86.
26   Ibid., p. 71.
27   Connolly, *Why I am Not A Secularist,* 1999, pp. 159–60.
28   Connolly, *Neropolitics*, 2002, pp. 85–86; Catherine Zuckert, *Postmodern Platos*, 1996, p. 88.

recognize the first cause, they are likely to ascribe another cause other than God as the first cause, with the result that they themselves might end up manipulating reality or others in a way that is unjust.[29] Immanent naturalism has some good points. It sees the importance of character formation. It also has the advantage of seeing life as a quest. It is willing to introduce a sense of wonder into human inquiry. Nevertheless, it is not willing to concede that anything concrete can come from this sense of wonder. It would always want to question, without accepting, any conclusions that one might make after one finds oneself in a sense of wonder.

Its chief defect is that it is not willing to put its confidence into a goal or standard that reason is meant to pursue. It also has a tendency to put confidence in reason on the same plane as religious belief. When we are engaged in a dispute between people of different beliefs, our only recourse is reason "to which all men are forced to give their assent."[30] This does not mean that any thinker who tries to understand the laws of nature and of nature's God has to categorically look down his nose at an immanent naturalist or even a Christian who does not believe that reason can lead us anywhere in our pursuit to understand the human person, politics, and God.

Looking for God is tough, "However, it is true, in divine matters the natural reason has its failings." Our intellect relates to divine knowledge as the eye of an owl to the sun.[31] Nevertheless, it is a worthy pursuit. Even popular songs recognize as much: "Mama always told me not to look into the eyes of the sun, but Mama, that's where the fun is."[32] It seems that not only do humans need to strive. They also need to strive for something or they tend towards despair or presumption.[33] It makes sense that eliminating the goal would lead those who eliminate the goal in the tendency of apathy, indifference, cynicism, and despair.

The immanent naturalist also wants to emphasize inquiry in the sensible realm. Here, the immanent naturalist might run the risk of mis-characterizing at least Aquinas's understanding of the inquiry by creating too sharp a division between the material and the immaterial or the sensible and the supersensible realm. Aquinas admits that inquiry into the sensible realm is hard, and that inquiry into the supersensible realm is even harder. The level of hardness does not mean that a person should give up the task or that the task is so easy that anybody who cannot successfully carry it out should be looked down on. Aquinas reminds us that we should not expect the task of reasoning about God to be easy. He is open to the possibility that our reason might not be up to the

---

29 *Summa Contra Gentiles*, II.3.
30 *SCG*, I.2.3
31 *SCG*, I.11.
32 Bruce Springsteen, *Blinded by the Light*.
33 *SCG* I.5.

task of inquiring into the intelligible characteristics of the most excellent substance.[34]

The arguments of the immanent naturalist, perhaps unwittingly, point to the
importance of virtue theory in public life and in academic pursuits. What the
immanent naturalist is searching for is understanding, friendship, and the seri-
ousness of respecting individual consciences. For a number of reasons, he thinks
that he does not see this in the way that current debates play themselves out in
the halls of academe and in the media. One might ask, if the halls of academe
are filled more with those who question the existence of God, would the lack of
understanding and friendship that they observe be a perception of the customs
they have created or those who have been excluded from the real creation of
those environments?

In the introduction to one of his books, Connolly speaks of the harrowing
experience he had as a young man being confronted by a fundamentalist in a
youth camp. This fundamentalist, from Connolly's point of view, coerced him to
accept Jesus as his savior. The ethos of engagement seems to want to limit the
possibility of such encounters from secularists towards Christians and non-sec-
ularists, but it still envisions micropolitics where the immanent naturalist seeks
out occasions to challenge theists and secularists. This can take place in church-
es, schools, the military and, I would add, dorms and bars. It would be good to
think of concrete examples that gives us something to really think about when
we think about micropolitics.

How would little moral experiments take place in a dorm or classroom that
would lead to a fugitive encounter of being? It seems that one of the dangers of
agonistic combat on the micropolitical level is that it risks violating the sanctu-
ary of conscience of each individual. Connolly properly criticizes the person
who somehow imposed on his conscience as a young man. It would be unfortunate if micropolitical agonistic deeds were to lead to the same thing happening
to the consciences of theists, atheists, agnostics, or even secularists. Each person has a domain of conscience that should not be entered into without the per-
mission of that person. To use any techniques, even artful ones, to enter into that
domain seems to go against a basic human instinct. When the immanent naturalist admits that he is playing a dangerous game, he seems to admit that there
is a way of thinking about persons that requires some standard for limiting what
one can or cannot do.

The point that one can derive from this discussion is that when a society has
a conflict between different beliefs that lead to people living their lives in different ways, for the sake of respecting consciences, understanding these different commitments, and fostering friendship among people it is good that we have
some standard that limits what a person can or cannot do in his or her political

---

34   *SCG*, I.3.4–5.

relationships with others. The theory of rights that we find in the Declaration is a good theory for understanding political relationships. We must look more closely at the Declaration to see how that theory relates to the natural theology of the Declaration.

The God of the Declaration

As we saw earlier, the Declaration of Independence has at least three important references to God, the God of nature, God the Creator, and the God of Providence. The contemporary political philosophers who see a natural theology behind these phrases, see the Declaration as under the influence of the political philosophy of John Locke. This political philosophy remains open to a link with natural theology, albeit with difficulties.

When the Declaration refers to the God of Nature, it speaks of God in as much as we can come to know Him through the use of human reason.[35] This doctrine is necessary for a country to orient itself politically. It is neither hostile to nor does it reject outright what a citizen might come to believe about God based on his or her faith. Nevertheless, it does not see faith in God as the proper footing for political life.[36] The Declaration also speaks of God as Creator. This understanding is important to understand how men relate to God and how they relate to each other. When it says that God is Creator, it establishes that God is the creator of intelligibility. It also establishes a scale of being and that humans have a place on this scale of being. Men are neither gods nor beasts on this scale. They are less than God, but equal to each other.[37] This has consequences for the way we think of rights and the way we think of political rule. Men do not have a right to rule over one another except by the consent of their fellow men. We are all equal, whether a statesman, farmer, or a plumber. The statesman can only rule over the farmer and the plumber if he gains their consent.

Finally, the Declaration speaks of God as providential, and according to our best lights on the question, this understanding of God as providential is accessible to all within the sphere of reason and natural theology.[38]

In summary, the Declaration has several statements which are the concluding statements of the natural theology of John Locke as expressed by the pen of Thomas Jefferson, with some slight additions of the Continental Congress of

---

35   Michael Zuckert, *Launching Liberalism: On Lockean Political Philosophy*, 2002, pp. 213–14.

36   Zuckert, *Launching Liberalism,* 2002, p. 215.

37   Zuckert, *Launching Liberalism* 2002, Jeremy Waldron, *God, Locke, and Equality: The Christian Foundations of John Locke's Political Thought*, Cambridge University Press, 2002, pp. 64, 79–80, 81–82.

38   Zuckert, *Launching Liberalism,* 2002, pp. 215–16.

1776. However, there are practical and theoretical difficulties that underlie the natural theology of the Declaration. One big one is how does the theory of rights in the Declaration relate to the natural theology of the Declaration. A further inquiry into Locke's natural theology and his political philosophy reveal these difficulties.[39] The authors who do comment on the philosophy underlying the Declaration see the difficulties in Locke's thought in two different ways, especially when considering Locke's theory in relation to concepts found in Christian revelation and theology. One line of thought presents Locke as relying on biblical ideas in order to establish the existence of God and the idea of equality. Another line of thought sees Locke's theory of rights as independent of his natural theology because he is not sure that his natural theology holds together.

According to one line of argument, it is necessary to root Locke's theory of equality in a religious foundation. It is not possible to bracket Locke's theology and build a secular conception of equality independent of his theology.[40] The unaided human intellect can establish the existence of God. It can do this because the intellect has the power of abstraction and because it can see the visible marks of a creator in the works of creation. Once it determines that God exists, it can ask if there are rules that follow on His existence. The intellect can relate the idea of God to the idea that there is a law that applies His conduct to the world. The atheist will have difficulty establishing the link between the existence of God and the rules of morality because the atheist will have difficulty identifying and using the power of abstraction. Thus, theological truth helps establish the link between God, the human person, and the rules of morality.

This argument at least relates to the truths we can come to by religious faith or even depends on biblical evidence and the teachings of Christ.[41] This theory of God and equality leads to a respect for conscience. Whoever holds it knows that he or she should be careful in how they treat others searching for the plans of Divine Providence. We refrain from hurting or exploiting anybody who is engaged in this mission.[42]

The picture of Locke's theory here sees Locke as developing a harmonious synthesis of ancient, medieval, and Enlightenment political theory. It might conflate the difference between natural theology and theology as they were traditionally understood.

A second line of thought attempts to explain the problem of natural theology and rights by showing the unresolved tensions that remain part of Locke's overall theory. This explanation sees Locke holding in tension an unconvincing natural theology with a separate theory of rights that might undermine the unconvincing natural theology. According to this line of thought, it is true that

39 Ibid.
40 Waldron, *God, Locke, and Equality,* 2002, pp. 13, 44.
41 Ibid., pp. 64, 66–67, 80–82, 96–97, 210–11.
42 Ibid., pp. 83–84.

Locke holds up the tradition about God and the natural law. He also remains open to the evidence from the Bible that supports his theory. Nevertheless, he is not sure that traditional natural theology or evidence from the Bible is a sure foundation for the practice of political life. So, he develops a theory of political society that does not depend on these two lines of the tradition. He leaves it to future scholars to determine whether the tension between this theory of political society can be reconciled with the arguments taken from tradition.

To begin, reason can lead us to knowledge of a creating, providential, and legislating God.[43] This proof is possible and from this proof we can deduce the will of God.[44] Once we know that a Creator has created humans, we know that humans belong to their Creator. If they harm or destroy each other they are harming or destroying another's property.[45]

While Locke gave a proof for the existence of a Creator, he was not sure that such a proof offered a sound foundation for political life. Neither Locke nor his contemporaries found his proof for the existence of God (a proof based on intelligent design) completely convincing.[46] Locke knew this and he thought in part that this showed that philosophy has difficulty identifying the laws of nature and the laws of ethics, and so philosophy as a whole will have difficulty convincing men of its ethical principles. In addition, Locke saw that ordinary men do not have the time or perhaps the capacity to follow the demonstrations of philosophers.[47] In addition to having its limits with respect to proving God's existence, Locke lacked confidence in the capacity of reason to know God as a revealer,[48] his lack of certainty that reason can know God as a legislator, and his realization that the ordinary man has neither the time nor the capacity to follow the demonstrations of philosophers led him to try to develop a different ethics as a foundation of social and political life.

Because Locke was not sure about his proof for the existence of God and its link to morality, he sought a less philosophical way to transform the beliefs held by the dominant world to improve the world in a physical, moral, and political way.[49] To do this, Locke created a theory of rights that would guide the institutions of a society. This theory relies on a certain understanding of God, with surprising results. Locke initially relies on idea of God as providential. However, he understands the providence of God in quite a different way than the biblical understanding of providence. According to Locke's understanding of

---

43 Zuckert, *Launching Liberalism,* 2002, 157, 189–92).
44 Michael Zuckert, *Natural Rights and the New Republicanism*, Princeton University Press, 1994, pp. 207–12.
45 Zuckert, *Launching Liberalism,* 2002, pp. 217–18.
46 Ibid., pp. 189–90.
47 Ibid., pp. 159–60.
48 Ibid., p. 141.
49 Ibid., p. 166.

providence, the person has a right to use the land to increase his wealth from it. Man desires to increase his land because he seeks his own preservation. The prosperity of the world is not the result of a gift of a providential God, but as the result of human labor, broadly understood. The material of nature is worthless when considered in and of itself. Man by his efforts makes something of value out of it. Man's need forms the real foundation of society.[50]

The natural law does not provide any limits on what humans can do to fulfill their needs. Late in the *Second Treatise*, Locke repeals all limits on acquisition, implying that humans do not belong to God, but to themselves.[51] They come to discover that they are self-owners through understanding themselves as self-conscious. Over time, the person experiences his intentions and actions as a person. He begins to possess data that indicate his consciousness and of his body. He bases his rights claims in the idea that he owns his body, not in a preexisting law.[52] This version of Locke, unlike the previous version, does not see natural theology or philosophy as the foundation for a political theory grounding the actions of persons in politics. Instead, it seeks such a foundation in the understanding of the person as a self-preserver, who preserves himself by acquiring property, working that property, and transforming it into wealth that he can use to fulfill his needs. Looking at Locke's thought as a whole, it seems as if Locke proposes a natural theology and remains open to the possibility of truth coming from revealed religion for the purpose of weaning his audience from its attachment to the idea of a transcendent natural law and making them more reliant on a theory of rights for engaging in political life.[53]

Both versions of Locke agree that he has a natural theology as part of his overall philosophy. They disagree to what extent Locke sees this natural theology as providing a basis for political society. The Declaration of Independence does not take a stand on the issue. Like Locke, it holds in tension the conclusions one might come to from a research into natural theology with a theory of rights that may or may not be able to stand independent of this natural theology. It has the advantage of remaining open to the possibility of a natural theology that has some link, however indirect, to the other branches of philosophy, including political philosophy.

Looking at the three takes that one could take on the Declaration, the immanent naturalist is suspicious of reason and of religious belief. He is also suspicious of a theory of rights that would exclude a theist or a nontheistic post-modernist from micropolitical discourse. The first Locke conflates religion and reason, but sees a Locke who is open to the influence of Christian belief on society, and that this is very much part of his theory of politics. The second Locke is

50   Ibid., pp. 143–45.
51   Ibid., pp. 191–92.
52   Ibid., pp. 194–95.
53   Ibid., pp. 162–64, 189–91.

not sure of the probability of natural theology and metaphysics, so he creates a theory of rights that would provide a new foundation. All three theories should be open to arguments of the existence of God from our natural understanding. Newman's arguments in *Grammar of Assent* that try to show God's existence from conscience and from the natural knowledge of religion could be put in fruitful dialogue with Lockeans and with post-modernists. Newman saw his own theory as an acceptance of, and response to, Locke on this point. All of these views, perhaps even Newman's, have the difficulty of finding a place for reason as exercised by the philosopher as part of political discourse. Newman's account of belief as it exists in the mind details how a person can go from one belief to the next, but he himself admits that he is leaving aside questions of metaphysics for the sake of showing the rationality of religious belief.

Conclusion

Any approach, however, that casts doubt on the possibility of reason reaching the truth, seems to put philosophy on soft ground. If we were to take this under-standing of philosophy and politics as representing all that can be attained in the pursuit of human wisdom, then the possibility of wisdom would be on soft ground. Perhaps it is useful in this regard to distinguish between the role of phi-losophy, including political philosophy and natural theology, as the pursuit of wisdom, and the role of political theory as establishing a basis for how political institutions will function. The former is more properly the domain of the teacher. The latter is more the domain of the teacher and the practitioner of the art of politics. The teacher of politics, as someone who tries to understand polit-ical life in as much as it relates to the other branches of human wisdom, would want to use reason to understand the highest and most divine things and link these teachings to what can be known about sensible reality.

There is also a need for theorists who develop ways of explaining how polit-ical societies emerge and of explaining what kinds of human behavior lead to healthy political institutions. This kind of inquiry will be more practical and will perhaps operate on principles less clearly reliant on the conclusions of natural theology or even of political philosophy. This does not mean that no link exists and that, therefore, the philosophical sciences should be excluded from the study of politics. Instead, it means that the halls of academe, and probably not the halls of Congress, are the best place to work out such problems.

Teaching politics in this way can help foster the respect for consciences, friendship, and understanding necessary for a healthy political community. For example, a teacher might explain to his class the various natural theologies con-nected to the Declaration of Independence. This offers the possibility of theists, atheists, nontheists, secularists, and lapsed theists of having some part in polit-ical life independent of what philosophical conclusions they might come to. It provides a standard of action that all can agree on and even sets out the limits that each party should respect when asking another person to consider its view of the world and to act on this view of the world. This teaching might not have much of a direct effect on students when they enter the Halls of the Congress and have to think through the public policy implications of whether to add an amendment to a bill, but each will be able to appeal to some understanding of rights that will lead him or her to respect the outcome and perhaps wait for a later day to seek an outcome more beneficial to his or her understanding of philosophy and society.

In other words, not all teachers can or should present a practical theory of how society functions or a practical theory of how to best understand and use the institutions present in a given society. In part, life itself takes care of that. At least some teachers of politics should present to students a reflection on politics and society that is at a remove from the ups and downs of political life and that is dialogue with the broader questions of human wisdom and the philosophical sciences. Such teaching does not exclude the possibility of creative thinking, but it does create a framework within which students will be able to understand their lives, including their political lives. Understanding the difficulties and attempts that have been made to overcome those difficulties (whether successful or not) can help students acquire a more moderate approach to life once they leave the halls of academe for the harsh realities of the political world. By teaching students that striving for divine things is difficult, and yet, that we should still strive for them can be an excellent safeguard against the kind of presumption, despair, or indifference that increases the possibility of violent ideological conflict or a meaningless life in pursuit of meaningless experiences.

The *Declaration of Independence* gives a framework for both, a political theory that enables citizens to act in common, and the hunch that helps political philosophers engage in further inquiries on the status of God in political philosophy. In this way, it remains an important document for study in the halls of the classroom and an important document for guiding the political practice of the ordinary man.

Ends, Acts, and God: Preserving Kantianism from Consequentialism

James Krueger

In "The Reasons We Can Share," Christine Korsgaard claims, "much of moral philosophy in the twentieth century" will look to later generations like "a struggle to *escape* from utilitarianism."[1] Interestingly, in the same article, Korsgaard appears to be open to the possibility that in the well-known case of Jim and the Indians, Jim may be justified in shooting one Indian to save the rest.[2] This might seem surprising for a professed Kantian. Here, I will argue that part of the explanation for this can be found in another article, "The Right to Lie: Kant on Dealing with Evil,"[3] where she presents an objection to a view she attributes to Kant. Ultimately, I think her objection fails as an objection to Kant, as does the view that she herself advocates in response to the objection. The reasons why, however, reveal a lot about the conceptual foundations of different ethical theories, and the role that belief in God must play in them. Ultimately, the conclusion I hope to suggest is that without belief in God, there is a deep problem that exerts an unavoidable pressure to accept some form of consequentialism. This pressure, then, can explain why Korsgaard stops short of endorsing universal moral rules against lying, suicide, and the direct killing of the innocent. Korsgaard may be right that the twentieth century will be viewed as a struggle to escape utilitarianism, but I think she is mistaken about what would be required to make that escape.

---

1   Christine Korsgaard, "The Reasons We Can Share: An Attack on the Distinction Between Agent-relative and Agent-neutral Values," in *Creating the Kingdom of Ends* (Cambridge: Cambridge University Press, 1996), p. 275, original emphasis, hereafter *TRWS*.

2   *TRWS*, page 296.

3   Christine Korsgaard, "The Right to Lie: Kant on dealing with evil," in *Creating the Kingdom of Ends* (Cambridge: Cambridge University Press, 1996), pp. 133–58. Hereafter *TRL*.

I. The Objection

The objection that Korsgaard presses against Kant in "The Right to Lie" stems from the consideration of particular cases. The central case she discusses is a familiar one, involving a murderer approaching one's door and asking if the person he intends to be his next victim is at home. The choice in this case is meant to be between telling the murderer the truth, that the person he seeks is at home next door (which will lead to the victim's death), and lying to the murderer in order to save the intended victim's life. Here I first want to consider a general problem that this case, and others like it, present for non-consequentialist ethical views. It is this general problem which is the basis for the specific objection Korsgaard presents. Then I will consider Korsgaard's objection to Kant in some detail.

What this case, and others like it, rely upon is that in each case the course of action normally considered to be morally forbidden (lying, or, in the case of Jim and the Indians, killing an innocent) is the only way to secure the outcome that a good person would most like to realize given the possibilities available in each set of circumstances (e.g., saving the potential murder victim, saving the most Indians possible).[4] In short, the case illustrates that it is possible for the ends we would like to seek, the ends that we believe a moral or virtuous person would seek, to pull apart from the actions that are normally thought to be moral or virtuous. This generates a problem in securing the intelligibility of the project of morality, of moral action as allowing us to achieve certain goods. If moral action cannot secure certain ends, ends that appear to be the best outcome of a given situation, then what is it that moral action aims at? What is moral action meant to secure for us if it cannot guarantee our fulfillment in this important respect? This thought, perhaps rightly, can lead to a rejection of the moral project as incoherent.

The problem related to one identified by Robert Adams. Consider one of several claims he thinks it is important to believe if we are to act morally. He thinks it is important to believe that a moral life is "better for the world."[5] We must believe that acting as we should does not, on balance, make the world a worse place. As Adams asks, "how else can we care about morality as morality itself requires?"[6] If morality can, and sometimes does, lead to disaster, how can we understand a universal call to be moral? What is important, then, about the cases Korsgaard considers is that in each, by acting morally, more evil seems to result, more death and more harm. Each makes it seems as if the course of action we are morally required to take is not consistent with our belief that morality is

---

4   This assumes, as is necessary given Williams intention in presenting the case, that there is no course of action that can save *all* the Indians.

5   Robert Adams, "Moral Faith," *Journal of Philosophy*, vol. 92 no. 2 (February 1995), p. 80.

6   Adams, p. 80.

good for the world. The problem is not one of providing a grounding for or justifying a moral requirement. The problem is maintaining the coherence of *action* in accordance with this moral requirement as seeking some genuine good.

Of course, one obvious solution to this problem is the consequentialist one. Consequentialism avoids the problem by defining it out of existence. By making consequences definitive of right action there can be no separation of the two, and hence no lack of fit to threaten the intelligibility of moral action seeking good ends. What is moral is always good for the world, by definition. The trouble with consequentialism, however, is that it seems to allow any kind of action, given appropriate circumstances; on simple consequentialism, there are no exceptionless moral norms, no actions that are always prohibited. To use Korsgaard's language, there is no point at which morality becomes uncompromising.[7] Korsgaard's hope is to find a position that can justify actions that violate certain general moral rules, without falling into a simple consequentialism.

II. Korsgaard on Kant

As mentioned above, the objection to Kant that I want to consider can be found in Korsgaard's article titled: "The Right to Lie: Kant on Dealing with Evil." It is more specific than the general problem I just mentioned, but ultimately stems from the same source. She objects to Kant because he holds strongly to certain moral rules, such as never kill an innocent or never lie, even if horrible consequences result. Korsgaard appears to believe that Kant's justification for doing this has to do with his claims about when agents can be held responsible for the outcomes that follow from actions.[8] She suggests that this claim about responsibility follows from his acceptance of a particular kind of ethical view, what she calls a *single-level* ethical view.[9] She distinguishes single-level ethical theories from two-level theories, asserting that a single-level view does not take into account *both* ideal and non-ideal cases, while a *two-level* theory does. There are two kinds of single-level view. They either (1) focus only on what a perfectly just society would be like (what is normally thought to be morally required of us in terms of the discussion above, never kill an innocent, never lie), or (2) focus only on the realities of injustice in the world that we are in (the outcomes given the nature of our world).[10] Two-level views attempt to do both, to "give us both a definite and well-defined sphere of responsibility for everyday life and some guidance, at least, about when we may or must take the responsibility of violating ideal standards."[11]

---

7   *TRL* p. 154.
8   See *TRL*, p. 150.
9   *TRL*, p. 147ff.
10 *TRL*, p. 147.
11 *TRL*, p. 150.

Korsgaard creates her Kantian two-level view by separating two of the formulations of the Categorical Imperative. The Formula of Humanity, she argues, is stricter and thus defines the moral ideal, while the Formula of Universal Law is more permissive and can provide practical guidance in the face of difficult, real world circumstances.[12] Thus, she claims, she can provide both a moral ideal to strive for, and practical guidance when faced with cases of injustice.

In contrast, Korsgaard claims utilitarian views are single-level in the second sense because they only focus on how to act in the particular circumstances we confront. Such views do not independently consider what we should do apart from outcomes; outcomes determine what is right.[13] Kant's view, then, is single-level in the first sense because, in her view, it focuses only on the ideal (never lie, never kill) and does not address the often less-than-ideal particulars of real cases (and because of this, there can be the lack of fit between what we should do, and what results, mentioned above). As she explains, "The standard of conduct [Kant] sets for us is designed for an ideal state of affairs, we are to always act as if we were living in a Kingdom of Ends, regardless of the possible disastrous results."[14] It is Kant's perceived inability to adequately respond to the reality of these disastrous results that leads Korsgaard to argue in favor of a two-level view.

By focusing only on an ideal state of affairs, she argues, Kant "defin[es] a determinate *ideal* of conduct to live up to rather than setting a *goal* of action to strive for."[15] As such, he gives the individual a "definite sphere of responsibility" such that "if you act as you ought, bad outcomes are not your responsibility."[16] Korsgaard considers this suggestion in relation to Williams' famous case of Jim and the Indians, and concludes that it is "grotesque" to argue (as she suggests Kant does) that Jim is justified in not killing a single Indian when this results in the death of 20 by simply saying that "[Jim has] done [his] part . . . and the bad results are not [his] responsibility."[17] It is this grotesqueness objection, then, that is at the heart of her rejection of a Kant-style single-level view and hence helps to explain her acceptance of exceptions to general prohibitions against lying, suicide, and killing of the innocent.

In response to this objection, I first want to consider whether the particular two-level theory that Korsgaard defends can meet the general challenge of making moral action intelligible as seeking some good without falling into

---

12   *TRL*, p. 151.
13   *TRL*, p. 149.
14   *TRL*, p. 149.
15   *TRL*, p. 150, original emphasis.
16   *TRL*, p. 150.
17   *TRL*, p. 150. I do not deny that Kant makes claims about responsibility that suggest this conclusion, what I object to is the thought that these passages can be taken in isolation, apart from arguments Kant gives elsewhere concerning the end of moral action. See below, p. 11ff.

consequentialism. Then I will turn to consider whether she is right to think that this claim about responsibility plays the role she identifies in Kant's ethical view. I will argue that she is not right in thinking this, and that there is a very different set of considerations that are key to understanding Kant's response.

III. The Problem with Two Levels

One danger that the proponent of a Kantian two-level view (such as Korsgaard's) must face is that of lapsing into the other kind of single-level view, lapsing into consequentialism. Korsgaard needs to provide an answer to the question of when it is okay to deviate from the strictures of the moral ideal without making a simple appeal to consequences. Such an appeal would threaten to transform the view into the other kind of single-level view. She recognizes this danger observing that the "common sense" answer to the question of when we can deviate is when the consequences of not doing so "would be 'very bad.'"[18] She rightly observes that this answer is both too vague and leads down a slippery slope to consequentialism (at any threshold, we can ask about cases just over the line and wonder why they are ruled out and others are not).[19] She claims that her own approach avoids both these problems.

Korsgaard suggests that she avoids consequentialism by providing a more clear, identifiable threshold at which consequences can become relevant.[20] Drawing on an example from Rawls, Korsgaard suggests that the point at which it becomes morally acceptable to trade gains in efficiency for reductions of liberty (for example) is the point at which inefficiency itself becomes a threat to liberty.[21] The suggestion seems to be that there is something special about this point, the point at which the consequences of acting in accord with a rule embodied in the goal we seek become so bad that they make the achievement of that goal impossible.

This seems like a promising suggestion, but it does not solve the problem, for it is hard to see how it generalizes to individual moral choices. Consider the case of Jim and the Indians. Jim is supposedly, in his specific circumstances, morally permitted to kill one Indian in order to save twenty. When we deviate from the ideal, Korsgaard argues, the ideal is not simply cast aside, but comes to define "the goal towards which we are working."[22] This is, then, how she can avoid the problem associated with maintaining the intelligibility of moral action with respect to ends. But how could it be that killing one Indian to save twenty aims at this ideal? How could we see this action as aiming at securing a world

---

18   *TRL*, p. 150.
19   *TRL*, p. 150.
20   *TRL*, p. 150–51.
21   *TRL*, p. 150.
22   *TRL*, p. 151.

in which this rule is universal? In fact, if we accept this threshold, we seem to be incapable of ever violating the ideal, for how can an action contrary to the moral rules contained in the ideal (goal) be a means for achieving a world in which such moral rules are always followed? The goal of deviating from the ideal, then, cannot actually be securing the ideal, if we are actually justified in deviating from it. But, if the goal must be something other than achieving the ideal, then the supposed threshold cannot be sustained. What makes this a unique threshold is that it marks where following the ideal causes problems with respect to the ideal. If we grant that causing problems with respect to some other goal is relevant, then we have started back down the slippery slope to consequentialism. It becomes hard to see why any important goal is not relevant, why any sufficiently bad outcome cannot justify a different course of action.

Rawls' example, dealing with broader social/political concerns, seems to be intuitively different from cases of individual moral choices. There is at least some plausibility to the claim that temporary injustice or restriction of liberty is necessary to set up the social conditions needed to secure greater liberty or equality in the long term.[23] However, it is not at all clear how killing an innocent man can be aimed at setting the conditions needed to make killing always immoral. How does killing one Indian serve to prevent another Jim at another time from finding himself in the exact same circumstances? How can committing suicide be aimed at making the world such that no one encounters the kind of profound suffering Korsgaard thinks can make suicide morally acceptable?

A second problem with Korsgaard's approach is that it does not provide a coherent *reason* for deviation from the ideal other than the recognition that the consequences of not deviating are "very bad." If there are no relevant factors other than consequences justifying deviation, there is no clear threshold to be drawn. To see this, consider again how she constructs the two levels of her account. As noted earlier, she relies on the claim that in some cases the Formula of Humanity of the Categorical Imperative is stricter than the Formula of Universal Law. This allows these two to define the two levels of the view; the former gives us the ideal, while the latter is responsive to the world.[24] Importantly, however, the arguments under the Formula of Humanity are perfectly general, they do not appear to admit the possibility of exceptions, so how can there be a reason for setting aside these arguments other than through the recognition that outcomes can trump any such arguments.

Consider, for example, the case of suicide. Korsgaard argues that Kant's argument against suicide under the Formula of Universal Law does not work,[25]

---

23   The claim here is tentative because it is not at all clear to me that Rawls' own examples don't fall victim to the same problem. The problem is, however, at the very least much more obvious in the case of individual morality Korsgaard discusses.

24   *TRL*, p. 151.

25   She suggests that Kant's argument relies on a certain teleological claim, that our instinct to improve our lives "cannot universally be used to destroy our life without

but that "Under the Formula of Humanity we can give a clear and compelling argument against suicide."[26] That argument is, simply, that "Nothing is of any value unless the human person is so, and it is a great crime, as well as a kind of incoherence, to act in a way that denies and eradicates this source of value."[27] She then claims that "it might be possible to say that suicide is wrong from an ideal point of view, though justifiable in circumstances of very great natural or moral evil."[28] In *The Sources of Normativity* Korsgaard further discusses the circumstances under which suicide becomes morally licit. It is when "[t]he ravages of severe illness, disability, and pain can shatter your identity by destroying your physical basis, obliterating memory or making self-command impossible."[29] The question, then, is how these considerations can provide a reason to deviate from the ideal that does not lead to outright consequentialism.

Notice that none of these considerations undermine or are even responsive to the argument given under the Formula of Humanity. It simply does not follow from the fact that nature can rob us of our identity that we are then justified in acting to destroy it. If it is indeed a "great crime" and incoherent to commit suicide in ordinary circumstances, to deliberately "eradicate the source of all value," then it still seems to be so in these special circumstances. To put the point another way, the fact that nature makes the achievement of a goal that we see as important impossible (in this case the preservation of our identity) simply does not make it coherent for us to act in a way that similarly makes the achievement of that goal impossible (committing suicide). The argument against suicide given under the Formula of Humanity does not admit to exceptions in such circumstances because such circumstances are, ultimately, irrelevant to the argument that is the basis for the rule.

Her suggestion, then, that sometimes circumstances can make suicide morally licit cannot be grounded in anything other than the claim that sometimes the badness of an outcome can override a moral rule. Since there is no threshold contained within the arguments for the rules themselves, the threshold must be found in the relationship of the outcomes to the rule. As we saw in the first argument above, however, Korsgaard's attempt to bootstrap a threshold from those considerations fails to make violating the rule coherent. All Korsgaard is left with, then, is the claim that the consequences are really bad and

---

contradiction" (*TRL*, p. 158n20). She does not believe such teleological claims have any place in the test associated with the Formula of Universal Law, and hence does not find his argument convincing. Further, she does not see any way, given her understanding of this test, to argue suicide is morally illicit (*TRL*, p. 158n20). Though I will not dispute her view here, I do not find her arguments convincing.

26   *TRL*, p. 152.

27   *TRL*, p. 152.

28   *TRL*, p. 152.

29   Christine Korsgaard, *The Sources of Normativity* (Cambridge: Cambridge University Press, 1996), p. 162.

no principled dividing line. Korsgaard thinks she can defend a threshold by holding to the Formula of Universal Law, but if really bad consequences allow us to violate the moral ideal (the Formula of Humanity), why can't the same consequences, or even worse consequences, allow us to violate the requirements of the Formula of Universal Law? Korsgaard insists that the Formula of Universal Law provides the threshold at which "morality become[s] uncompromising" but she cannot give a principled defense of this claim.[30] And with no threshold, there is only a very slippery slope to consequentialism.[31]

---

30   *TRL*, p. 154. Further, it is worth noting that the general problem of securing the intelligibility of an action with respect to ends is not entirely solved simply by moving to a two-level view (even if it could be defended). The moral ideal, remember, is the goal when we are justified in deviating from the strictures of the goal, but what is the positive goal that we seek when the bad consequences of an action in accord with the ideal fall just short of allowing us to deviate? Might there not be some cases where following the moral ideal leads to bad, but not quite bad enough, consequences? How do we secure the intelligibility of action in accord with the ideal in such circumstances? Say Jim must choose between executing one Indian and watching twenty be tortured (but not killed)? Or between killing one and watching the twenty be separated from their families and children with no hope of ever returning? What is the positive good we seek in such cases? Notice, importantly, that the goal cannot be the ideal itself, for if the ideal is the goal when we act according to the ideal (not just when deviating), then Korsgaard cannot generate her grotesqueness objection in the first place. There would no longer be a need simply to deny responsibility for the bad outcome, because there would be an overriding of a positive good that one is seeking. This thought is, I hope to argue, the heart of Kant's own solution to the problem.

31   In a footnote, Korsgaard further expands on why she believes nonideal theory, theory which gives guidance as to how we should act in imperfect real-world circumstances, does not become a kind of consequentialism (*TRL*, p. 157n15). She offers two basic reasons. The first is that the goal is "not just one of good consequences, but of a just state of affairs." The second is that "the ideal will also guide our choice among nonideal alternatives," again providing a constraint other than simple good action in the choice of a course of action. In the first case, the problem with Korsgaard's claim is simple. What I have argued above is that the nonideal theory in fact recommends a course of action that is inconsistent with the sense of justice embodied in the just state of affairs, so it is hard to see how that just state of affairs could be the goal of the action in question. It is not that the ideal has the wrong sorts of characteristics, it is that the action in question seems incompatible with seeking the goal embodied in the ideal. This same problem undermines her second response. If the nonideal theory recommends a course of action incompatible with the moral view embodied in the ideal, it is hard to see how the ideal could be understood as guiding our choice. If it did, it would seem to force us to reject the suggestion of the nonideal theory.

IV. Kant's Solution

Let us consider, then, Kant's own account, and see if it cannot do better. Korsgaard clearly thinks that the only solution which Kant offers is the simple assertion that the bad consequences that follow from moral actions cannot be seen as the responsibility of the person who has acted morally. I believe, however, that there is much more to his answer. Either the claim about responsibility is not meant to provide a candidate end, in which case it cannot solve the problem, or it does propose a candidate end that is clearly inadequate given Kant's own view. If we take the avoidance of responsibility to be the end that is sought, then the action is no longer consistent with the requirements of the moral law. If Jim's action aims at avoiding the dirtying of his own hands, then he is using the Indians as a means, a means to secure his own good conscience. Aiming at this end in these circumstances is, in fact, incompatible with the requirements of the moral law so it cannot serve as the end that is sought when we act from the moral law. Kant can rightly say that acting in this way is grotesque, not because of the consequences that result, but because it is immoral to do so. If this is Jim's end, then his action cannot be motivated out of respect for the moral law.

Korsgaard is right to think that the solution of the problem requires identifying some goal, some good that moral action seeks. Kant's claims about responsibility, then, cannot solve the problem because they do not provide an appropriate positive goal for moral action. Not just any end will serve as a solution to this problem of ends. The concern is that in cases such as those under consideration here, there appears to be no connection between moral action and an *appropriate* end. In such circumstances, remembering Adams' phrase, morality does not seem to be good for the world. Limiting responsibility does not solve the problem because aiming at this cannot be seen as aiming at a genuine good for the world.

What, then, is Kant's answer? The only way to solve the problem is to provide an end, something that can rightly be viewed as a good that is sought through moral action even if other, bad consequences also result. In this way, acting morally can still intelligibly be understood as seeking some good, even in such difficult circumstances. The place where Kant talks about the end of moral action in most detail is in the third *Critique* under the rubric of the highest good. There he claims that there is an end that we seek when we act morally. He calls this end the *highest good* and suggests it is constituted by both the requirements of the moral law and happiness, where the former is the condition for the achievement of the latter.[32] Since he does not believe happiness and morality are

---

32　Immanuel Kant, *Critique of Practical Reason* (Cambridge: Cambridge University Press, 1997), 5:110–11. Page references to Kant will be to the standard German Academy edition pagination.

connected by definition, since the concept of morality does not imply happiness, the only possible way these two could be connected is for them to be causally connected.[33] For Kant, then, when we act morally we seek the highest good; we seek a world in which moral action is connected to the achievement of our ends as a causal condition for that achievement.

Importantly, then, Kant suggests that the moral rule is constitutive of the good that is sought in such a way that this good cannot be sought by any means other than moral means. We fall victim to irrationality if we seek a world where moral action is a condition for the achievement of our goals by acting immorally. In such a case we would be willing, at the same time, that we achieve our goal and that it be impossible for us to achieve our goal by the means we have selected.[34] It is, of course, important that Kant thinks this is the *highest* good. The end that is sought must be the greatest good, the complete, unconditioned end so that this end is always capable of securing the intelligibility of moral action in terms of ends. If some end could be higher than this, then the problem could be reconstituted in cases where an immoral act is the only way to secure this higher good.

The problem, however, is that simply asserting that moral action must have this relationship with the good that we seek does not completely solve the problem. As the cases Korsgaard considers suggest, there are some circumstances where moral action seems unable to achieve the goals we seek. More generally, there is no guarantee that living a moral life will lead to a good life.[35] People who always act morally suffer calamities just like everyone else. Why should someone who has faced one calamity after another when acting morally continue to act morally when he can achieve other good ends by not doing so? Why should Jim act morally when he knows that he could save the lives of so many Indians if, in this case, he sets aside his moral commitments?

It is to this very real problem that Kant responds by introducing the practical postulates. We must, according to Kant, believe in God (or at least *a* god capable of securing the connection between moral action and the ends we seek) and the immortality of the soul (so that there is time for this connection to be realized).[36] In this way, we can see the possibility of moral action connecting up

---

33   Kant, 5:111ff.

34   The reason Korsgaard's view falls victim to the first objection I mentioned above is because she appears to endorse this same view of the relationship of the goal and moral rule in cases where deviation from the ideal is acceptable. In such cases, the moral ideal becomes the goal. She then tries to suggest that this goal can be sought be means inconsistent with the moral rules that are part of the goal, but this, I argued above, cannot be made intelligible.

35   Obviously, "a good life" is taken to mean something more than doing what is morally required; it also implies happiness or fulfillment.

36   Kant, *Critique of Practical Reason*, 5:122ff. Korsgaard does acknowledge, in passing, that Kant responds to this problem in this way, but she never discusses in detail

with the ends that we seek, and the intelligibility of the project of morality in terms of ends can be secured. Rather than trying to make clear the reasoning here in purely theoretical terms, let me introduce a further example.

Consider the Maltese conjoined twins treated in England in the year 2000 and referred to in the press by the names Mary and Jodie. There are several reasons for selecting this case, but the most important are the fact that it is a real world case, not a philosopher's thought-experiment, and that it is comes about naturally, that is it does not rely on a person acting immorally in order to generate the problem (unlike the other cases mentioned so far). The twins presented a moral dilemma because they were joined in such a way that even though Mary had all her own vital organs, her heart and lungs were not capable of circulating and oxygenating her blood. An artery connecting Mary's circulatory system to Jodie's heart was all that kept Mary alive. Unfortunately, Jodie's heart, while strong enough to support her own life, was not strong enough to support Mary's as well. Doctors believed that Jodie's heart would only continue to function for a matter of months before it gave out and both twins died.[37] The choice, then, was a difficult one: separate the twins and kill Mary, or do nothing and watch both Mary and Jodie die.[38]

How do we see our way through such a case, to a description of choosing not to separate the twins such that it can be understood as aiming at an appropriate end? Notice first that this case does fit the general problem we have been considering. Acting in the way normally thought to be moral (avoiding direct killing) does seem to lead to more suffering, more death. It does, then, seem that moral action, in this case, is not consistent with believing morality is better for the world. In response, Kant suggests that this apparent problem is just that, an appearance. If we understand what morality requires of us properly, we see that

---

the viability of this response, nor does she show how it might relate to the considerations of responsibility mentioned above. See *TRL*, p. 149.

37 The British Court of Appeal nicely summarizes the details of the case in the introduction, summary and conclusions of the decision in the case. The case number was B1/2000/2969, and the decision was released on September 22, 2000.

38 I will assume without argument, though I think there are compelling arguments that can be given, that the separating of the infants would be a case of directly killing Mary to save Jodie. I do not want this discussion to get bogged down in questions of double effect and the moral importance of the distinction between killing and letting die, which are interesting in their own right, but have no bearing on the point I want to make here. I will assume, for the sake of this discussion, that separating Mary and Jody would count as a case of direct killing – although I know this is controversial. Presumably we could imagine a similar case where saving one life really did depend on directly killing another as a means to that end. The possibility of such cases arising independent of the evil actions of some human beings is all that is required to support the argument here.

not only does moral action aim at some good, but it is the only way to achieve this good.

We have also seen, however, that not just any good will do, there are certain requirements that the end must meet. As pointed out above, for example, the goal of avoiding responsibility will not serve because it is not a genuine good for the world and is not compatible with the moral law. Further, if we note that the prohibition against killing is founded on the requirement that we recognize the value of other beings like ourselves, we see that this end cannot serve since this end is not an end for the twins.[39] It is not properly part of the project of their lives, so taking this end does not seem to be consistent with aiming at a good for them. Since either course of action clearly causes harm to one or both, the fact that this end is not an end for them makes it impossible to see the action as consistent with the belief that their lives are valuable. Following the rule for this reason, then, would be to act contrary to the very basis for the rule.

The only way to avoid this problem is for the end to be an end for them as well, something that can be genuinely viewed as a good for them. We have, then, four requirements that the end must meet: 1) right action must be constitutive of it, 2) it must be a possible end for those affected by the action, 3) it must rightly be seen as good for the world, and 4) it must be plausibly seen as the highest, or most important, good. Kant takes what he calls the highest good, a world in which moral action always results in achieving the goods sought, to be one such end. Other possibilities include union with God or human flourishing. In each case, it is plausible (or necessary) to claim that the end can only be sought by right action, the good that is sought is a good for all human beings, and its achievement is good for the world. Each of these ends, then, is a candidate for what we seek when we act morally.[40]

The fact that such action results in the deaths of both Mary and Jodie, however, must be reckoned with. Since it results in their deaths, it seems impossible to see the moral action (or failing to act) as seeking these goals *for them*. Even when the end sought could be, in general, an end for them, the fact that it results in not only harm but death makes it hard to see how it can be an actual end for them in this case. But notice that this is only true if what we are concerned with

---

39   Whatever reason we have for valuing the lives of other human beings, whether it is because they are rational, created in God's image or whatever, the requirement to act in a way that recognizes that value still remains.

40   The fact that each of these ends are ends for Mary and Jodie is important, because only in this way can we see seeking this end as not using them to achieve an end. Since in each of these cases, the end sought is also the ultimate end for them, we are furthering their projects as much as are own, we can see this end as consistent with seeking their fulfillment. As will be argued in a moment, however, more needs to be said before this claim can be fully made good.

is life in this world.[41] Kant argues that we must believe the soul to be immortal, so that there is an infinite period of time in which persons can move toward the highest good.[42] Even with an infinite amount of time, however, the world seems to be such that we will be frustrated. The goal itself does not always seem to be achievable, given the world that we experience, because of the way moral action and the ends we seek can pull apart. Nature simply is not such that we can avoid such frustration even with infinite time. Believing in the possibility of achieving such a goal, then, similarly depends on believing in the possibility of a God capable of arranging the world such that the goal is possible.[43] For Kant the end in question is something that we just do seek, in so far as we are moral beings, so there is no separation between our seeing this end as important for Mary and Jodie, and their own seeking of it. Both stem from the same source. In so far as we are morally obligated to encourage moral action on the part of others, then, we are morally obligated to see this as a possible end for them, a part of their project.[44] It is also important that for Kant following the moral rule is itself necessary for actually making progress towards achieving such a moral, transcendent end because the end is itself partly constituted by the moral law itself. This precludes the possibility of achieving the end in question by any means other than moral means.[45]

If we admit a transcendent dimension to human life, then, we begin to see the possibility of acting in a way consistent with seeing the lives of Mary and Jodie as valuable, their projects as in some sense our own, valuable to us, even when our failure to perform the surgery results in the death of both infants.[46] The special relationship between the rule and the ends in question, as illustrated in the case of Kant, explains why this end can only be sought by following the rule, and underscores the necessity of following the rule even when we focus attention on the ends of action, and not on the rule or the action itself. Since not

---

41   Notice that it is not the value of their lives that needs to be secured, it is the need to *recognize* or, perhaps better, *acknowledge* the value of their lives *through our action*. This does not mean that life in this world is not important, not good, or cannot be seen as such without admitting the possibility of an afterlife. All it means is that in this case, we need to see the possibility of there being a further good in order to make our action intelligible as seeking a good for them given what results from the moral course of action.

42   See Kant, *The Critique of Practical Reason*, 5:122 24.

43   See Kant, *The Critique of Practical Reason*, 5:124–32.

44   In fact, more than just a part of their own project, but the ultimate end of their life.

45   These arguments are here phrased in terms of Kant's own theory, but I believe they apply equally well to other non-consequentialist ethical views that can meet the challenge discussed here.

46   The problem is not finding value in their lives, but acting in a way consistent with recognizing that value.

performing the surgery results in the death of both Mary and Jodie, the only way to sustain the intelligibility of the project of morality is to see their projects, their lives, as not limited to the material world as we experience it. In short, it is to believe in the possibility of God's existence and of the immortality of the soul.

Though the end that Kant selects (the highest good) is particular to his own ethical view, the central move can be generalized. I have already mentioned two other candidate ends (flourishing, relationship with God). In each, moral action must be constitutive of the ends that we seek, to make it impossible to achieve what is thought to be good by any means other than moral means. That good must, of course, be general – it must be good for those affected by the action and good for the world in general, given the arguments we have seen here. Nonetheless, the heart of the solution is the assertion of this strong connection between what is right, and the good we seek. The problem that leads to the need for belief in God, then, can also be generalized.[47] We simply have no reason to believe that such a connection is born out as we act in this world. Right actions pull apart from the achievement of good ends and threaten the intelligibility of moral action as seeking such ends. The only solution is to look beyond this world, to look beyond to something capable of transforming the world and securing the connection that is needed.

V. Conclusion

As we have seen, then, there is a general problem in making moral action intelligible as action for ends. It is important that what we believe to be right connects up with the ends that we seek. We have also seen that there are several possible ways of thinking about this connection.

First, we could think that what achieves the ends that are important *to us* defines what is right; this is the consequentialist solution and avoids the problem by defining it out of existence.

Second, there is Korsgaard's approach, which attempts to maintain that sometimes moral action is important to the fulfillment of the ends we seek, but sometimes the fulfillment of our ends should allow us to deviate from what is ordinarily considered right. The challenge for this view, as we have seen, is to provide a principled distinction of cases. Korsgaard's own attempt, as we have seen, fails. It is worth wondering if any such account could succeed. On what principled basis could consequences define what is right only sometimes? If we have a principled defense of a moral rule, how can we make consequentialist

---

47 Of course, in the case of Aquinas, the end explicitly acknowledges the need for God, so no further argument is required. In his case, this argument only highlights why reference to God is a necessary part of that end.

exceptions to it without admitting that consequences are playing the defining role? How can we hold fast to any rule, if no rule connects up with ends in the way required?

Third and finally, we can think that what is right is of necessity a condition for our achieving the ends that we seek. For Kant, right action is what makes us eligible for, deserving of, achieving our ends; as with most modern virtue theorists, human flourishing cannot be achieved through immoral action. In the world we inhabit, however, we can come to have reason to doubt whether this connection between morality and happiness can be realized, whether we can indeed achieve our desired end through right action. No matter how often we do the right thing, it can seem that the ends we seek will not be fulfilled; sometimes, as in the cases important here, suffering appears to be the only possible result. Since the connection between morality and happiness does not seem to hold in the world we experience, but belief in its possibility is crucial to maintaining the intelligibility of morality in terms of ends, taking this solution requires the belief that the world we experience is not how the world has to be, that it is not all that there is to the world. In other words, since we must believe in the connection between morality and happiness, but cannot secure that connection for ourselves, we must believe that God can secure it for us.

In other words, it seems that ethical theory is faced with a fundamental choice: either accept some form of consequentialism, or hold on to hope that there is a God who can, in the next life if not in this, secure the connection between good ends and moral actions.[48]

---

48 Portions of this paper appeared earlier in "The Practical Importance of Moral Teleology," in *Teaching, Faith and Service: The Foundation of Freedom*, Rev. William Hund, C.S.C. and Margaret Monahan Hogan eds. (Portland: University of Portland Press, 2006), pp. 179–86.

ETHICS ON ONE WING

Laura L. Garcia

Several contemporary devotees of atheism offer moral theories that purport to capture the substance of morality within a world-view explicitly committed to materialism. The recent entries in this category share the view that many of the ethical norms endorsed by religious believers, especially Christian believers, are pernicious and should be eliminated. That is, their goal is not to develop a naturalistic moral theory that will justify traditional moral norms, but rather to develop a theory that will justify replacing these norms with more "progressive" or "enlightened" moral principles. I consider here three such anti-theistic theories along with some criticisms of each approach. Finally, I propose a renewal of metaphysical inquiry as crucial to sustaining a sound and persuasive natural law ethic.

Three Naturalist Proposals

(I) *Nielsen's New Blend for the Nineties*

Canadian philosopher Kai Nielsen published a book in 1972 called *Ethics Without God*; in 1990 the book reappeared under the same title, revised and greatly expanded. The earlier version simply endorsed a consequentialist moral theory directly, but sometime in the 1980's Nielsen tried to convert to a Rawlsian theory, with mixed success. Nielsen's current moral theory proposes a Rawlsian methodology of *wide reflective equilibrium* which he describes as follows:

> We start with firmly fixed considered moral judgments such as . . . the belief that religious or racial intolerance is unacceptable, that promises must not be broken, that we need to have regard for the truth, that people are never to be treated as means only, and the like. Starting with these considered moral convictions that we hold most firmly, we see whether we can arrange them into a coherent and, of course, consistent package. We should also take the extant moral theories and see how well they match with these considered

judgments. The relation is much like that of scientific theories to observed experimental data. . . . The theory that squares best with and explains best this consistent set of confidently held considered judgments is, *ceteris paribus*, the theory we should accept.[1] This approach sounds relatively harmless at first blush, apart from who is included in the "we" with reference to whose considered moral judgments we must square a moral theory. This is no idle concern, as becomes apparent when Nielsen describes the data set he has in mind. "*Wide* reflective equilibrium must not only seek the most coherent fit possible between considered judgments and moral theories; it must also seek the most accurate account available to us of the nonmoral facts (if that is not pleonastic); and the best social, scientific, and philosophical theories we have."[2] Nielsen wastes no time in letting us know which philosophical theories count as the "best" in this context. "Many Christians believe that under all circumstances suicide is wrong, abortion is wrong, and pre-marital intercourse is wrong. . . . According to some Christians, God categorically forbids suicide and so they conclude that suicide is wrong. But . . . there are serious and deep questions about whether the concept of God is a coherent concept and, beyond that, even if we can make sense of the concept, there is still the problem of whether there is a God or whether belief in God is rationally justified."[3]

Nielsen does not pause to consider whether prohibitions against suicide, abortion, and premarital sex might be derivable from one of his own "considered judgments," for instance, the claim that persons are never to be treated merely as means. Instead, he criticizes those believers who ground moral judgments in divine commands for failing to justify the ontological claims implicit in their theory. What it takes to justify these deeper claims is assumed to be (minimally) arguments for the existence of God and for the rationality of belief in God.

Nielsen does acknowledge the existence of a natural law tradition in ethics and notes that some have even accused him of adopting a natural law approach (horrors!) with his appeal to considered moral judgments. Of course, Nielsen's version lacks the rational foundation for these judgments provided by Aristotle or St. Thomas Aquinas. In fact Nielsen rejects any grounding of natural law in human nature, not by offering arguments against this approach but by asking several rhetorical questions about it: "How do we know that there is one thing – happiness, beatitude, or whatnot – that is the *rationale* of all rules of

---

1   *Ethics without God: Revised Edition* (Buffalo: Prometheus, 1990), pp. 19–20.
2   Ibid., p. 21.
3   Ibid., p. 24.

reason? . . . Even if there is only one such end, how do we know it is happiness or beatitude?"[4]

Oddly, some of Nielsen's criticisms do more to support than to undermine Thomistic natural law theories, as when he claims that "one cannot just somehow see what is good through becoming aware that there is a supremely powerful and intelligent creator of the world."[5]

Presumably, this is the point of developing a moral theory and not stopping with cosmology. Nielsen himself describes natural law theory as grounded in a common humanity and in a common quest for happiness/beatitude, not solely or directly in the existence of a perfect God. Be that as it may, his final verdict is that "the Thomistic conception of the natural law is a myth."[6]

Why a myth, as opposed to merely mistaken or naive or, as Alvin Plantinga might put it, epistemically sub-par? Nielsen senses the looming presence of God in the background of most natural law theories, no doubt, as well as the presence of such disturbing entities as immaterial souls with free agency – and these are ruled out by his prior commitment to materialism.

Turning to Nielsen's own proposal for an ethic without God, we are hardly surprised to find that it remains in this second edition a version of consequentialism, oriented toward fulfilling basic human desires and interests of varying sorts, maximizing the satisfaction of these desires to the greatest extent possible for all humankind. Nielsen starts with judgments about what things are intrinsically good, based on that fact that we pursue them for their own sake. His list includes happiness, self-consciousness, and a sense of self-identity. Presumably happiness (even if it is interpreted here simply as pleasure or as the satisfaction of one's desires) is a strong candidate for an intrinsic good. Though Nielsen frets over is-ought problems, he also admits that "any realistic morality – secular or religious – links in some close way with what men on reflection actually desire and with that elusive thing we call human happiness."[7]

But why self-consciousness? It is a condition for happiness, but so are many other things – that one is alive, that the nature remains uniform, and so on – and self-consciousness cannot be an end of action (unless we count drinking a lot of coffee, or maybe popping acid). Self-identity is more puzzling still – can anyone fail to be self-identical? In any event, the only absolute moral norm in Nielsen's theory is consequentialist: "Actions, rules, policies, practices and moral principles are ultimately to be judged by certain consequences: to wit, whether doing them more than, or at least as much as, doing anything else or acting in accordance with them more than, or at least as much as, acting in

---

4   Ibid., p. 29.
5   Ibid., p. 31.
6   Ibid., p. 35.
7   Ibid., pp. 91–92.

accordance with alternative principles, tends, on the whole, and for everyone involved, to maximize satisfaction, that is, to maximize happiness, minimize pain, enhance self-consciousness and preserve one's sense of self-identity."[8]

Though Nielsen is mildly troubled by the charge that consequentialism fails to ground any other exceptionless moral norms, he bites the bullet here and claims that there are "hard cases" where doing evil that good may come is not only permissible but even obligatory. Some of these cases are eerily relevant in today's climate. For instance, certain acts of terrorism that target innocent people are said to be justified by their effects, when no other means of achieving the aims of the terrorist group present themselves. "In certain, almost unavoidable circumstances, they must deliberately kill the innocent," Nielsen says. "In [the film *The Battle of Algiers*] Algerian women – gentle women with children of their own and plainly people of moral sensitivity – with evident heaviness of heart, planted bombs that they had every reason to believe would kill innocent people, including children."[9] One might have thought that a moral theory that clashes so loudly with our considered moral judgments would have to be abandoned, but not so. Nielsen is content to make exceptions to these judgments for the sake of maximizing satisfaction for the greatest number. While some homage is paid to Rawls' notions of equality and fairness in order to block some of the more shocking implications of consequentialism, it is consequentialism that wins any conflict between principles of justice and the perceived greater good.

Against Elizabeth Anscombe's defense of moral absolutes, Nielsen claims that insisting on allegiance to a moral law even when it involves great sacrifice for oneself and others can itself be a "morally monstrous" position, since evaluation of actions should always involve choosing the lesser evil (he thinks). Consider the moral principle Nielsen endorsed at the beginning of his book – that persons must never be treated as instrumental to an extrinsic end. As the book progresses, this bold principle dies the death of a thousand qualifications – it turns out that (1) the fact "that a normative ethical theory is incompatible with some of our moral intuitions (moral feelings or convictions) does not refute the normative ethical theory;" (2) the Kantian norm about respect for persons only requires that we treat them *initially* as equally deserving of respect, instrumentalizing them only with great reluctance; and finally (3) we do not treat a man *only* as means to an end in, say, whacking him to save the rest of us, as long as we don't single him out because of anything peculiar to him and we have "humane reasons" for acting as we do,[10] (presumably these reasons aren't humane toward Jones, but you can't have everything).

Would the existence of God in the metaphysical background of these

---

8   Ibid., p. 129.
9   Ibid., pp. 130–31.
10   Ibid., p. 144.

questions give one pause in setting aside fundamental moral convictions? In effect, Nielsen agrees that it would. Citing John Hick's description of the moral life endorsed by Jesus, Nielsen concedes, "If the creedal and doctrinal claims of Judaism or Christianity were true, then it would indeed be rational to act as Hick's believer is convinced we ought to act [that is, in imitation of Christ]."[11] (Hick's article is from 1959, a time when *Hick* still thought the creedal and doctrinal claims of Christianity were true.) Naturally, this move cannot rescue moral absolutes for Nielsen, since he thinks "we have no evidence at all for believing in the existence or love of God."[12]

It's a little difficult to see how Nielsen's blend of intuitionism, consequentialism, and Rawlsian liberalism holds together in the end. More importantly, it is hard to see how he can maintain a role for moral truth within the naturalistic framework to which he is committed. He proposes that a moral principle is true if it is required by "the moral point of view," which involves adopting Nielsen's consequentialist axiom enjoining maximal satisfaction of desires and interests, as long as we treat every person's interests with the same moral weight.[13] As to why we should adopt the moral point of view, and whether this point of view is itself reflective of truths about the world, the only reason given is that societies need a moral code in order to have something higher to appeal to than the positive law and the will of the majority. That a moral theory is socially useful in this way hardly entails that it is true. To the extent that persons in a society agree to adopt this particular moral point of view, presumably there can be some *agreement* about moral principles, but this falls short of showing that Nielsen's moral point of view is rationally justifiable.

Pragmatic considerations come into this adoption decision because of a failure to ground a consequentialist moral theory in anything else. Nielsen's appeal to *wide* reflective equilibrium is no accident, since he uses the metaphysical assumptions of current materialist views to rule out moral theories inconsistent with these assumptions. If we bring to our consideration of the ethics a prior commitment to physicalism and determinism, it is no surprise that Thomistic natural law theories don't make the cut. Theoretical support for materialism is hard to find in Nielsen's book, except for a brief (nostalgic?) reference to the verification criterion of meaning. If this criterion were revived, however, Nielsen's own commitments to happiness and equality would fare no better than Aristotle's commitment to eudemonia. The moral intuitions he appeals to could

11 Ibid., p. 98.
12 Ibid. The argument for this claim is that "none of the proofs works," including the argument from religious experience. Nielsen can't seem to stop himself from bringing in the verification criterion of meaning here as well: "Our troubles are compounded when we realize that we do not even know what we would have to experience for it to be true or even probable that God exists." (p. 99)
13 Ibid., p. 197.

not serve as raw data, revisable or no, since they would be considered strictly meaningless by positivist empirical standards. In the end, says, Nielsen, he cannot give us a good reason to choose his moral point of view; it is a matter of simply choosing it.

(II) *Moore's Objectivism Lite*

Michael Moore, a living philosopher not to be confused with G. E. Moore, hopes to find a place for moral realism and objective moral norms within a moral intuitionist theory along the lines of that offered by (confusingly enough) G. E. Moore. Michael Moore treats "good" as an impersonal, natural quality that we postulate to be present in some objects and actions. In a 1996 collection of essays edited by Robert George called *Natural Law, Liberalism, and Morality*, Moore considers this question: "Would the existence of God help at all in justifying our belief that morality is objective? Would God's existence strengthen the case for morality's objectivity?"[14] His answer is that it would not, and he ultimately suggests that God's existence might be incompatible with morality's objectivity.

Moore defends a position he calls moral realism, a two-fold metaphysical claim that "(a) moral qualities such as goodness, wrongness, etc., exist . . . and (b) the existence of such moral qualities does not depend on what any person or group of persons believes about them."[15] For Moore, moral qualities are natural properties of things, and facts about which activities, relations or states are good to do or good to be in are simply evident to us. One cannot ground their moral value in anything further, including any facts about human nature or human desires. "Rather, our actions, relations, or states possess the quality of goodness, a quality existing in the universe like wetness,"[16] and human actions need not be the only things in the universe that possess this quality, according to Moore. If a work of art has the property of being good, then it will be good whether or not there is any beholder in the universe (God included). Values are to be completely independent, in Moore's view, not just of person's *beliefs* but also of their needs, desires, ends, or motives. Values are not simply mind-independent, then, but wholly impersonal for him.

On the other hand, Moore wants moral truths to do some work in guiding our actions and choices. "If an action is morally right, or a state of affairs morally good," he says, "necessarily we have an objective, non-prudential reason to pursue it."[17] How this is supposed to follow in Moore's theory is difficult to see.

---

14   "Good without God," *Natural Law, Liberalism, and Morality* (Oxford: Clarendon, 1996), pp. 224–25.
15   Ibid., p. 222.
16   Ibid., p. 256.
17   Ibid., p. 256.

As Jorge Garcia asks in a critical response to Moore's article, "What makes
value give people reasons to act if that value has no necessary connection to
what advances any person's goals, projects, plans, needs, purposes, or function?"[18] Moore's version of moral realism goes well beyond the claim that the
good is independent of *what people believe about the good* to the claim that it
is independent of people altogether. Perhaps a duty to pursue various goods is
itself based in the value attached to this action, and we can recognize this. In
addition to apprehending the goods in the universe, we also apprehend that we
ought to pursue these goods. (Much still needs attention in this theory, however. What counts as pursuit here? Maximizing the goods? Maximizing the pursuit
of them and minimizing violations against them? Are there norms for adjudicat-
ing conflicts, and do we intuit these as well?)

   While G. E. Moore compared "good" to a simple, unanalyzable quality like
"yellow," Michael Moore compares "good" to "wetness," but neither thinker
succeeds in finding a common reason to apply the term "good" to items as
diverse as a movie, a computer, a sniper, and an afternoon.[19] "Good" isn't like
yellow or wetness, but we can often tell what qualities *make a thing good* or
what is *good for that thing*. It's just that these qualities will not be the same in
every case. Be that as it may, suppose we grant Moore's view of values as non-
natural qualities, and go on to ask, as he does, whether the existence of God (as
Christians describe God) would make any difference to ethics. Michael Moore
deeply opposes divine command theories of ethics, but recognizes that there are
other ways in which God's existence might be relevant to moral theory. In his
critique of Moore, Jorge Garcia details some advantages that could accrue to
one's moral theory if God exists.

> (1) God's existence helps justify the overriding importance of moral consid-
> erations over prudential considerations. God can ensure that acting rightly
> or virtuously will not lead to unredeemed calamity for a person.[20]

> (2) God's existence helps justify the existence of absolute moral norms that
> admit of no exceptions. The theistic picture includes the claim that God
> loves human persons for their own sake. That human persons should learn
> to love others (and God himself) is his primary goal for us. The *motives and
> intentions* behind our actions are the focus of moral judgments then,

---

18   J. L. A. Garcia, "'Deus sive Natura': Must Natural Lawyers Choose?" in *Natural
     Law, Liberalism, and Morality*, ed. Robert George, p. 276.
19   In a long footnote, J. Garcia reminds us of Aristotle's argument against the Platonists
     of his own day who thought that there was a univocal "form of the good" involved
     in every ascription of goodness to anything. Aristotle also criticizes the view that
     there is a univocal form involved even if we restrict ourselves to what is intrinsical-
     ly good. (See Garcia, op. cit., pp. 280–81).
20   Ibid., p. 272.

whereas the *consequences* of our actions matter only indirectly (e.g., we need to know what foods a baby can handle if we are trying to help and not harm her).[21]

(3) Theism grounds a view about human dignity, derived from the claim that every person has been willed by God and has a destiny in God (or at least in the contemplation of God). Theism thus "helps immunize us against the modernist view that morality consists merely in placing constraints on the individual's pursuit of what is taken to be the basic business of life – satisfying his desires (nowadays dressed up in Rawlsian garb as 'living according to his own conception of the good')."[22]

(4) Theism explains how objective values can have a place in the world of "facts." It presents the world of facts as already pervaded by value, since this world comes from, reflects, and returns to, the source of all [worldly] facts in the reason and will of God.[23]

The grounding of absolute moral norms was a problem for Nielsen's theory and it turns out to be an equally grave problem for Moore. He tries to show that God's existence does nothing to increase the gravity or weight of agent-relative considerations in morality (the agent's attitudes, intentions, character, and the like). If God wants each person (equally) to conform to the moral laws, Moore asks, what about a case where my conforming to the law will result in others violating it? "What sense can we make of one Being, who, though he cares for each of us equally, doesn't care to minimize moral failure or maximize moral success?"[24] Moore assumes that what God wants is to minimize the total number of times moral laws get violated – i.e., that God would be a consequentialist. But suppose that what matters to God instead is that persons become virtuous and loving and attain their ultimate end, not that they strive to bring about the greatest balance of moral success over moral failure (as if anyone could realistically make this a personal goal). Then God would not endorse deliberately committing an evil that good may come.

While an explicit appeal to theism is not necessary for coming to *know* that there are some absolute moral norms, it can be difficult to show *why they should not be compromised* in the face of so-called 'hard cases.' Moore believes (I take it) that deliberately taking the life of an innocent person (murder) is wrong, incest is wrong, torturing prisoners is wrong. But he denies that moral norms can be captured in "text-like formulations" like "Do not kill." One must grant exceptions to this rule, for killing in self-defense, in defense of one's family, as a

---

21   Ibid., p. 273–74.
22   Ibid., p. 274.
23   Ibid., p. 275.
24   Moore, p. 244.

soldier in a just war, and so on, and "new exceptions will always be in principle discoverable."[25] Moore seems oblivious to any common elements in his list of exceptions or of the need to rule out pseudo-exceptions (killing because we are really, really mad). He concludes that there is no finite proposition that can capture moral principles – stated in propositional form, they can only be guidelines as to what is *prima facie* right or wrong. Just as in Nielsen's theory, one can be morally obligated to violate a fundamental principle to prevent great enough harms or promote great enough goods. Moore confidently opines that "one who would not kill or lie to save his family is in no sense a saint, but rather, a kind of misguided moral leper."[26] Similar considerations apply to incest. "We might come across (actually or imaginatively in literature) incestuous relationships that enhance the dignity of persons in ways we had not anticipated. [!] In which event we might withdraw our initial judgment that incest is even *prima facie* wrong."[27]

Moore defends his version of moral realism on the grounds that it is "the best explanation of various facets of our common moral experience. This is a fallible, scientific inference, not an unseemly leap of faith."[28] God is not needed to make sense of this experience, according to Moore. Even so, why the hostility toward theistic moral realists? Shouldn't they (we) be seen as allies? Well, no, as it turns out. "My own metaphysics . . . is to refuse to countenance the existence of objective moral qualities unless they cause other (non-moral) entities, qualities, and events to occur, and such a causal role can exist for moral qualities only if they supervene upon, and in some sense are identical to, non-moral (i.e., natural) properties. . . . Nothing in this kind of ethical naturalism should shock empiricist sensibilities about what can exist."[29]

In other words, Moore is committed to a materialist view of the world, and believes that while values exist, this is only because they are identical (on an item-by-item basis) with empirical properties of some kind. Values do no causal work – one may not be able to translate value language into value-free language, since the claim is not that value is itself (as a category) reducible to or identical with some empirical quality. Moore's reductionism is rather a reduction at the level of particulars, so that one cannot neatly replace universal concepts about value with empirical concepts having the same extension. The analogy is with mind-brain identity theories in philosophy of mind; since it proved impossible to replace mental language with physical language, now the proposed identities are at the level of individual mental states and individual brain states. Moore claims his theory is still a form of realism, since values are independent of

---

25   Ibid., p. 243.
26   Ibid., footnote 69, p. 267.
27   Ibid. For Moore's treatment of the norm against torture, see his article "Torture and the Balance of Ends," *Israel Law Review* 23 (1989), pp. 281–344.
28   "Good without God," p. 260.
29   Ibid., p. 232.

minds and their beliefs. On the other hand, they turn out to be identical with natural qualities and have no causal role to play, so that *qua* values they are in effect
eliminated. For most philosophers, this would count as anti-realism about values. It is hardly obvious, then, that Moore has succeeded in preserving a role for
objective moral principles in a world view committed to the non-existence of
God, souls, and libertarian free will.

(III) *Pinker's Blue Genes*

The psychologist Steven Pinker stands out among popularizers of the evolutionary paradigm as the key to understanding nearly everything there is to know
about human beings and their behavior. The key assumption of this approach is
a view of the human mind as identical with the brain, and the brain as having
evolved to its present state over vast millennia by way of random variation and
natural selection (with or without "punctuations" that cause major leaps in evolutionary development). As Pinker puts it in the preface of his 1997 book *How
the Mind Works*: "The mind is a system of organs of computation designed by
natural selection to solve the problems faced by our evolutionary ancestors in
their foraging way of life."[30] This assumption opens up a new discipline in the
academic world, evolutionary psychology, which claims to find the physical
causes (in the evolutionary history of the human race) that lie behind virtually
every emotion, belief, and practice of human beings.

A difficulty for this new science is that it hardly seems to qualify as a science at all. Claims about the evolutionary path behind specific emotions (such as
altruism, sympathy, etc.) cannot be tested, or can only be tested in a very wide
sense of that term. It's a matter of some amusement that those who rose up with
indignant horror to condemn creationism as non-scientific are seldom found cru-
sading against evolutionary psychology. The field is riddled with the *post hoc
ergo propter hoc* fallacies, since the fact that certain conditions obtained in the
distant past that *could* perhaps account for current human beliefs, desires, etc.
does nothing to show that these conditions were in fact the cause of those beliefs
or desires. Even apart from the disputed notion of agent causation, one could
attribute a large role to environmental and cultural factors in explaining a person's
behavior and outlook. Instead, neo-Darwinian theories of human nature attribute
nearly every such factor to the genes – and the "goal" of our genes is to repro-
duce themselves; they are "selfish" genes. If we care about our children, it is due
ultimately to our interest in preserving our genetic legacy. If we tend toward
depression, this will have a genetic explanation – perhaps in term of "blue" genes.

As for moral beliefs, these are taken to reflect various human emotional
reactions to different objects and practices, reactions that contributed at some

---

30   Pinker, *How the Mind Works* (New York: W. W. Norton and Co., 1997), p. x (preface).

point to the survival of the individual or of the human species. As emotions, they are neither true nor false. "People have gut feelings that give them emphatic moral convictions, and they struggle to rationalize the convictions after the fact."[31] Moral convictions about what is good and bad, right or wrong, can have no objective or realist basis. Moral reasoning is nothing more than rationalization. We assume that Pinker will go on to embrace moral nihilism or non-cognitivism (since there are no moral facts in this view). Instead, he endorses consequentialism as the one moral theory that reason would recommend.

> The difference between a defensible moral position and an atavistic gut feeling is that with the former we can give *reasons* why our conviction is valid. We can explain why torture and murder and rape are wrong [perhaps he should check with Michael Moore about torture and murder], or why we should oppose discrimination and injustice. On the other hand, no good reasons can be produced to show why homosexuality should be suppressed or why the races should be segregated. And the good reasons for a moral position are not pulled out of thin air: they always have to do with what makes people better off or worse off, and are grounded in the logic that we have to treat other people in the way we demand they treat us.[32]

It is remarkable that Pinker can know that promoting people's welfare and following the Golden Rule are grounded in reason, while other moral principles are dismissed as rationalizations of gut feelings. As it turns out, even the Golden Rule quickly succumbs to consequentialist considerations, since making people better off turns out to be mainly a matter of making oneself better off – others are out of luck.

It is probably unfair to criticize Pinker for the numerous philosophical blunders in his books, which are often entertaining and illuminating and are directed to a popular audience. What is shocking (to me, anyway) is Pinker's constant appeal to what 'most scholars' or the *cognoscenti* are saying as in effect a demonstration of a claim. Consider the many authorities and luminaries that appear in the following citation: "For millennia, the major theories of human nature have come from religion. . . . But the modern sciences of cosmology, geology, biology, and archeology have made it impossible for a scientifically literate person to believe that the biblical story of creation actually took place. As a result, the Judeo-Christian theory of human nature is no longer explicitly endorsed by most academics, journalists, social analysts, and other intellectually engaged people."[33] Those who do continue to accept something like the

---

31   *The Blank Slate: The Modern Denial of Human Nature* (New York: Penguin, 2002),
     p. 271.
32   Ibid., pp. 274–75.
33   Ibid., pp. 1–2.

Judeo-Christian theory of human nature come in for ridicule and contempt in later chapters of the book. (Leon Kass and President George W. Bush are particular targets here.) On the other hand, while Pinker is (we assume) scientifically literate, how confident can he be about the sweeping metaphysical claims he makes in the passage just cited?

Those of us of a certain age (i.e., 45 and up) might be reminded of a television commercial featuring the actor Chad Everett, who played a doctor in the series "Marcus Welby, M.D." The ad was for a medical remedy, perhaps a painkiller, and Everett began: "I'm not a doctor, but I play one on TV . . . ." No one listened to the first part, because for us viewers he was a doctor. We saw him in thoughtful, capable, and compassionate action every week. A similar illusion is created by Pinker's list of respectable people who have jettisoned theism. Pinker is not a philosopher, but he does play one from time to time in his popular writings, without providing any careful arguments for his metaphysical claims or making much effort to capture accurately the views he attacks. Nor does he tell his readers that there are some well-informed and thoughtful people on the other side.

When Pinker turns to a consideration of particular moral judgments, his main concern is to eliminate moral absolutes and to completely erase moral prohibitions against the favored projects of current scientists – in vitro fertilization and cloning – and the favored practices of the cultural elite, especially sexual practices. Moral absolutes are dismissed as efforts to "treat an act in terms of virtue and sin as opposed to cost and benefit," when we should all know that considerations of virtue and vice are "morally irrelevant grounds."[34] Two examples Pinker mentions in the realm of sexual ethics are incest (apparently a favorite for atheist moral theories these days) and, of all things, sex with a chicken. He assures us: "Many moral philosophers would say that there is nothing wrong with these acts, because private acts among consenting adults that do not harm other sentient beings are not immoral."[35] Mention of sentient beings might lead to some concerns about the chicken, but let's pass over that issue for the time being.

Pinker cites a psychological study of a decade ago that asked people to justify or explain the strong reaction of disgust they felt when presented with various scenarios involving incest, bestiality, and the like (eating your dog was another example – he is already road kill and you need the food). Initially, respondents to the survey focused on negative consequences of these acts, whether immediate or delayed, and on offenses to the wider community. If they were told that none of these negative consequences would (or did) happen in these cases, they were hard pressed to find a further reason for their moral

---

34   Ibid., p. 277.
35   Ibid., p. 271.

disapproval. They would say things like "I don't know; I can't explain it, I just know it's wrong."[36] The psychologists take this to indicate that there is no rational foundation for such moral claims, apart from a consideration of consequences – the cost/benefit model. But one might instead take seriously the respondent's insistence that they "know it's wrong," even when told that the wrongness can't lie in the negative effects of the action.

What grounds this deeply held moral conviction? Perhaps in the case of the sex examples, people believe that these offend against personal dignity, that they are degrading of oneself and others, that such acts cannot be sought as genuine goods for us, and so on. Knowing that the scientists will reject any such claims, they fall silent instead. The claim that human persons are inviolable, that they cannot be instrumentalized, grounds many of the moral principles that come under attack in *The Blank Slate*. Prohibitions against abortion, against auctioning orphans to the highest bidder among prospective adoptive parents, against harvesting organs from living people who are not going to live much longer – none of these survives the cost/benefit test. A typical treatment of these issues appears in Pinker's endorsement of *in vitro* fertilization: "As recently as 1978, many people . . . shuddered at the new technology of in vitro fertilization, or, as it was then called, 'test-tube babies.' But now it is morally unexceptionable and, for hundreds of thousands of people, a source of immeasurable happiness or of life itself."[37] It is also a source of death or suspended animation for hundreds of thousands of other people (at the embryonic stage), but this fails to register on Pinker's cost/benefit scale. Why is the death of these small persons not counted at all, even if only to be overridden by a so-called higher good?

The answer can be found in a telling passage on the morality of abortion, wherein Pinker shows his devotion to materialism and scientism. "The idea that ensoulment takes place at conception . . . flouts the key moral intuition that people are worthy of moral consideration because of their feelings – their ability to love, think, play, enjoy, and suffer – all of which depend on a functioning nervous system."[38] This is the kind of claim that can take your breath away. People are worthy of moral consideration because of their feelings and their abilities alone. What justifies Pinker's fundamental claim about human nature? The answer is: nothing. A materialist picture of reality, including humans, interpreted through the lens of evolutionary biology, yields no discernible moral theory. Hence, those operating from this perspective either simply assert some initial axioms to get the system going or, as in Moore's theory, pretend to accept "values" into a system that has no place for them. Pinker thinks morality can

---

36 Ibid., p. 270. The study referred to is: J. Haidt, H. Koller, and M.G. Dias, "Affect, Culture, and Morality, or Is it Wrong to Eat Your Dog?" *Journal of Personality and Social Psychology* 65 (1993), pp. 613–28.
37 Ibid., p. 274.
38 Ibid., pp. 225–26.

survive just fine in this modern day in which all thinking people agree with him about human nature as a product of a blind watchmaker. Some of us will continue to have our doubts, however.

A MODEST PROPOSAL

Thomists and other advocates of the natural law share the view that some substantive moral claims are objectively true (correspond to a mind-independent reality) and that these are accessible by the use of human reason (independently of knowledge of special revelation). There are differences over what *kinds* of moral claims can be grounded in this way, the *ground* or *warrant* for the claims, and the *way they are known*. Many Thomists follow Aristotle in presenting claims like "Rational activity in accordance with virtue is the highest good for humans" as accessible to reason, grounded in human nature, and knowable by broadly empirical methods.[39] Some more recent advocates of the natural law begin from practical reason, hoping to derive theoretical claims (such as "Knowledge is a basic good" and "Never choose directly against a basic good") from the principles we use to make rational or intelligible choices. The movement from one to the other is not logically necessary, but is thought to be obvious to the normal, unbiased, reflective person.[40] Finally, some natural law theorists ground substantive moral norms in self-evident, necessarily true basic principles that are held to be accessible to every rational person.[41] The differences among these approaches to natural law are significant in many respects. One of the most important, I believe, lies in their respective implications for the role of metaphysics in moral enquiry. A natural law theory that begins with a theory of human nature clearly requires a defense (at some point) of that theory of human nature, and this in turn may require a defense of related metaphysical claims. The latter kinds of natural law theory seem to make no such initial appeal to human nature or to other claims about the world, apart from the moral judgments themselves.

---

39 Ralph McInerny develops this view in various contexts; one very accessible summary is his *Ethica Thomistica: The Moral Philosophy of Thomas Aquinas* (Washington: Catholic University of America Press, 1982).

40 Such a theory has been proposed by Germain Grisez, John Finnis, Joseph Boyle, and Robert George. For a brief statement of this position, see Robert P. George, "Natural Law Ethics" in Philip L. Quinn and Charles Taliaferro, eds. *A Companion to Philosophy of Religion* (Cambridge, MA: Blackwell, 1997), pp. 460–65.

41 For a statement of this theory, see Hadley Arkes, "The 'Laws of Reason' and the Surprise of the Natural Law" in Ellen Frankel Paul, Fred D. Miller, Jr. and Jeffrey Paul, eds. *Natural Law and Modern Moral Philosophy* (Cambridge University Press, 2001), pp. 146–75. Arkes links his theory to that of Thomas Reid, a contemporary and critic of David Hume.

Metaphysics, conceived of as (in part, at least) the study of what kinds of things are real in addition to those accessible to the five senses, finds few defenders in philosophical circles these days (and fewer still in the broader intellectual community). It is generally assumed that optimism about efforts to know what there is cannot survive attacks from positivism, scientism, hermeneutics, historicism, anti-realism, the purveyors of the paradigm-shift, and so on. Advocates of these anti-metaphysical positions also oppose one another, of course, but conventional wisdom is that they are the current players in the marketplace of ideas and it is bad form to offend all of them at once.

The current situation has discouraged philosophers of a metaphysical bent from pursuing traditional metaphysical questions guided by reason and common sense. At best, someone might venture a claim about what our ways of speaking commit us to, or what are the features of our conceptual scheme. As to whether these ways of speaking and thinking reflect genuine truths about the world, contemporary philosophers are often loathe to say. Some of this is attributable to sheer survival tactics, since in the publish-or-perish atmosphere of the academy, it ill behooves one to proffer views that one's colleagues will universally condemn, not merely as mistaken, but as hopelessly naive, ridiculous, uninformed – in effect, an embarrassment. Safer by far to focus on the interpretation of a text, the description of a language game, or tracing the implications of a philosophical claim in a purely hypothetical way. (*If* it were accepted, *then* these claims would also have to be accepted, given a greater probability, etc.)

The aversion to metaphysics and the desire to dissociate oneself from its intellectual odiousness affects other parts of philosophy as well. Moral and political theorists increasingly aspire to operate in the open air, as free as possible from substantive metaphysical commitments. Strategically speaking, this approach has something to recommend it, since a moral theory may thus gain a fair hearing even from those deeply opposed to metaphysics itself or to the metaphysical claims lurking in the shadows of the normative theory. The goal would be to delay discussion of divisive deeper issues and focus on claims that are closer to the surface – the moral judgments themselves, or the attendant epistemological claims. One might try to display the coherence and explanatory power of the moral theory vis-à-vis our moral intuitions taken as "raw data," prescinding from the question of where these intuitions come from and whether they have any rational force.

I have no intrinsic objection to such approaches. But it is increasingly clear that substantive *metaphysical truths* lie at the foundation of substantive *moral truths*, and that the metaphysical task cannot be postponed indefinitely. Indeed, it becomes even more urgent today in light of escalating assaults on human dignity from reproductive technologies and from social forces in a culture riveted to self-gratification. Showing that the moral prohibition against murder is absolutely binding is itself no piece of cake in today's climate, but at least there is a general societal consensus against murder. More difficult to defend are absolute prohibitions against the use of IVF technologies, cloning, contraception, homosexual acts, same-sex unions, and so on. The clear and present danger to oneself or others is less obvious in these cases, and our society tends to support scientific innovations and look the other way with respect to what their neighbors are doing. (Smoking is the exception here, as is having "too many children.")

In light of these realities, I believe we should undertake a renewed study of metaphysical problems, accompanied by a robust realism and a deep respect for reason and common sense. With respect to anthropology, it might be promising to develop a metaphysics of human nature that draws on both the Aristotelian/Thomistic understanding of man as a rational, social animal and the relational, personalist themes of Pope John Paul II. The goal would be to build a persuasive and substantive metaphysical foundation for natural law ethics, particularly where ethics addresses human sexuality. While some philosophers find substantial, perhaps irresolvable, tensions between the common sense methodology of Aristotle and the phenomenological methodology of personalism, it is obvious that John Paul II sees these two approaches as compatible and even complementary. A clear and carefully argued view of human nature and the dignity of persons is, I believe, the only permanent intellectual defense against the current assaults on human dignity.

Although advocates of natural law sometimes begin elsewhere in attempting to ground substantive moral claims, this does not render a theory of human nature unimportant for their own projects. Beginning from practical reason and the kinds of goods we choose for their own sake can perhaps lead to claims about what humans see as fulfilling for them or as necessary to their flourishing. But if it the materialist picture of human beings is correct, this project will appear to be nothing more than a catalog of human desires acquired over years of evolutionary development, not a reason to endorse a particular group of desires as ultimate or to take their rational grounding as anything more than an elaborate rationalization. By the same token, an intuitionist moral theory generally assumes that the moral sense is a rational faculty leading us in the direction of truth, and that basic moral judgments are common to all rational persons. Both claims are hotly contested, and both can be better supported within a theistic metaphysical outlook that includes some account of human nature such that the basic principles available to conscience can be supported by attending to the kind of beings we are.

In his masterful encyclical on faith and reason, Pope John Paul II opens with this beautiful image: "Faith and reason are like two wings on which the human spirit rises to the contemplation of truth."[42] In seeking the truth about

---

42 John Paul II, *Fides et Ratio* (Boston: Pauline Books, 1998), p. 7 (the opening paragraph).

morality, reason is greatly helped by faith, even if neither the mysteries of faith nor the existence of God is presupposed in natural law theories. Nearly everyone begins with the moral intuition that the dignity of human persons is inviolable, but secular moralities seldom retain it in the end. Most people begin with a belief in an immaterial dimension of the self, and in free will as the basis of moral responsibility; without faith, one can be tempted to surrender these metaphysical claims and so destroy the very foundations of morality. I am a firm believer in the possibility of developing a sound natural law ethics without explicit appeal to articles of the faith. But when philosophical ethics explicitly rejects God and embraces naturalistic materialism, natural law theory does not have a prayer. Two wings are better than one, even if you can make it with one; and if we attempt to do morality without metaphysics, we won't even have a whole wing – maybe just a few feathers.

Public Discourse without God?
Moral Disposition in Democratic Deliberation[1]

David Thunder

According to Richard Rorty, the American nation was founded on a "happy, Jeffersonian, compromise" reached between the Enlightenment and the religious, "making it seem bad taste to bring religion into discussions of public policy."[2] Whatever we may think about the historical accuracy of this claim, it seems fair to say that not only in the U.S., but also in most European nations, it is often considered at best inappropriate, at worst offensive and ignorant, to bring up religion or religious considerations in the context of a discussion of law or public policy. In recent decades, liberal political philosophers have offered a variety of moral and pragmatic rationales for principles of religious restraint in public discourse,[3] and if their arguments succeed, then they appear to validate the popular suspicion of religious interventions in debates about public policy and law.

However, arguments for religious restraint have not gone unchallenged. A rich literature has, in fact, effectively exposed a deep incoherence in the liberal

---

1   I would like to thank Matt Mendham for some helpful editorial and philosophical comments on an earlier draft of this paper. Thanks are also due to the late Prof. Phil Quinn for leading some very stimulating discussions on this and related subjects in a philosophy graduate seminar at the University of Notre Dame in the Spring semester of 2003.
2   Richard Rorty, "Religion as Conversation-Stopper", *Common Knowledge* 3, (Spring 1994): 1–6, 2.
3   See, *inter alia*, Robert Audi, *Religious Commitment and Secular Reason* (Cambridge: Cambridge University Press, 2000); Kent Greenawalt, *Private Consciences and Public Reasons* (New York: Oxford University Press, 1995); Bruce Ackerman, *Social Justice in the Liberal State* (New Haven and London: Yale University Press, 1980); John Rawls, *Political Liberalism*, The John Dewey Essays in Philosophy (New York: Columbia University Press, 1996); Rorty, "Religion as Conversation-Stopper"; Gerald F. Gaus, *Justificatory Liberalism: An Essay on Epistemology and Political Theory* (Oxford and New York: Oxford University Press, 1996); Thomas Nagel, "Moral Conflict and Political Legitimacy", *Philosophy and Public Affairs* 16, 3 (Summer 1987): 215–40.

principle of religious restraint. Arguments for restraint are both logically self-defeating (given the wider liberal commitments of their proponents) and morally and politically untenable.[4] But much of this criticism remains within the boundaries of liberal discourse. In this paper, I aim to move beyond the liberal model of discourse by interrogating its underlying assumptions and investigating positive alternative approaches to discourse. I begin by reviewing the established criticism of religious restraint, and suggesting that underlying it is a deeply inadequate understanding of the nature, dynamics, and goals of public discourse. I then propose a more plausible approach to discourse by turning attention away from the regulation of speech *content* and towards a fuller account of the *virtues* required for a vigorous and civil public conversation. Finally, I return to the issue of religiously-informed public discourse and offer some reflections on this contentious issue, in light of my virtue-centered model of discourse.

The Failure of Liberal Arguments for Religious Restraint

A principle of religious restraint holds that citizens ought to refrain from advancing arguments for policies and laws that depend for their validity upon religious claims, that is, claims derived from religious tradition or authority, theological doctrines, or some form of theism. Rather than catalogue all the arguments that have been made on behalf of such a principle, I will here construct an argument that draws on some of the most representative and convincing positions in the literature. The broadly liberal quest to justify a principle of restraint has two main components: first, a liberal conception of respect for persons; second, a liberal view of the preconditions of social stability.

---

4   My arguments against religious restraint are inspired by a rich literature and it would be unduly cumbersome to acknowledge my intellectual debts at every step of the argument. The following have been particularly helpful: Nicholas Wolterstorff's arguments in the book-long debate, Robert Audi and Nicholas Wolterstorff, *Religion in the Public Square: The Place of Religious Convictions in Political Debate* (London: Rowman & Littlefield Publishers, Inc., 1997); Michael J. Perry, *Love and Power: The Role of Religion and Morality in American Politics* (New York and Oxford: Oxford University Press, 1991), and Michael J. Perry, "Why Political Reliance on Religiously Grounded Morality is not Illegitimate in a Liberal Democracy", *Wake Forest Law Review* 36, (Summer 2001): 217–49. I would especially refer the reader to the enlightening debate conducted in the *San Diego Law Review* in Fall 1993, including Jeremy Waldron, "Religious Contributions in Public Deliberation" (817–48); Michael J. Perry, "Religious Morality and Political Choice: Further Thoughts - And Second Thoughts – on Love and Power", (703–27); and David Hollenbach, "Contexts of the Political Role of Religion: Civil Society and Culture" (877–901).

According to the liberal conception of *respect*, no reasonable and rational adult should be required to do something with the backing of physical force unless the coercion can be justified to him in terms he can understand and could, in principle, accept. That is, coercive measures must be justified in terms that could be seen to be reasonable from the perspective of the coerced. This is because to treat a person with respect is to address oneself to the person's *reason* and *free will* rather than forcing the person to conform to a scheme or purpose that is entirely foreign to her and irrelevant to her own subjective purposes and interests.

Obviously, it is not easy to pin down precisely what is meant by the term "reasonable" and what it means to say a proposal *could* be seen as reasonable from the perspective of a coerced person. Within the liberal tradition exemplified by Rawls, a proposal, in order to be reasonable, would need to fulfill two basic conditions: on the one hand, it would have to be *rational* in the sense of meeting a certain threshold of logical coherence and proposing means to ends that bear a real relation to human interests. Secondly, it would have to be *reasonable* in the special sense of being sensitive to the interests of others or being minimally motivated by a sense of justice. To say that a proposal could be seen to be reasonable by the coerced is to say that assuming the coerced person is capable of pursuing and revising a conception of the good (i.e. is "rational") and is capable of having and acting upon a sense of justice (i.e. is "reasonable), that person could accept the proposal without converting to a different worldview or "comprehensive doctrine."[5]

Of course, this notion of accessibility or reasonable acceptability raises many questions. For example, what precisely would it be mean to say that the grounds for a coercive law "could be" accepted by the coerced? I think we must seek for an answer in Rawls's notion of the "burdens of judgment," the fact that given people's differing views of the world and their diverse personal experiences or life histories, their moral and political judgments – even when reasonable and motivated by upright moral intentions – can vary dramatically. Such variation is not due to faulty reasoning, malice, or "unreasonableness" but rather, due to the "burdens of judgment" – the fact that people are inescapably conditioned in their judgments by a background of habits and experiences, many of which are beyond their control.[6] Given the burdens of judgment, on

---

5   This discussion mirrors Rawls's treatment of the "reasonable and the rational" in *Political Liberalism*, 48–54 (hereafter '*PL*'). Rawls stipulates that by a "fully comprehensive" doctrine is meant a philosophical or religious view that "covers all recognized values and virtues within one rather precisely articulated system; whereas a "partially comprehensive" doctrine "comprises a number of nonpolitical values and virtues and is rather loosely articulated" (*PL*, 152, n. 17).

6   For a more detailed account of the burdens of judgment, see PL, 56–57. The burdens of judgment include complexity and scarcity of evidence; deciding what

what basis am I to override another person's judgment about what is in his best interests, or how he is to live his life? It must be on some basis that a reasonable person, even with his present epistemic "baggage," could come to see and accept. Does this mean that I must secure the actual agreement of every reasonable person? This requirement would be so strong that it would rule out a whole host of laws that are widely viewed as reasonable and necessary for the common good. The point of finding accessible grounds, then, is not to secure immediate and unqualified approval of those grounds or the law they are supporting, but to offer reasons that "hook in" fairly obviously to the worldview or shared reason of my interlocutor, and do not blatantly bypass his epistemic horizon. For example, if I argue that such-and-such a vaccination should be required since I believe public health is a top priority at this time, a person may reject my prioritization of public health and may even think that requiring vaccinations does not follow from such a priority, and yet consider my proposal as "accessible" to her, as addressed to our shared reason, and as accepting, rather than overriding, the burdens of judgment. This example shows that the accessibility requirement interpreted in light of Rawls's "burdens of judgment" need not require a high degree of consensus on actual policy outcomes, and is therefore not as politically naïve as it might at first appear.

But *to whom* are arguments to be accessible? To all citizens? No, for that would be far too strong a requirement. Rather, to all *reasonable* citizens. But what is a "reasonable" citizen? One helpful definition of a "reasonable" person is a person who is willing to live a spirit of reciprocity in his dealings with other citizens.[7] This means that he is willing to offer his or her fellow citizens fair terms of social cooperation, and is sensitive to the burdens of judgment. Sensitivity to the burdens of judgment entails an awareness that people can reach different positions based on different experiences and judgment calls, without necessarily opening themselves to (justifiable) moral condemnation. If a person has abandoned the notion of seeking fair terms of cooperation or demands that everyone else see the world through her own epistemic horizon, that person has essentially rejected the liberal conception of respect and therefore lacks the moral requisites of liberal citizenship. He or she can safely be

---

weight to assign to various considerations; the problem of interpreting or applying abstract concepts and criteria; unique life experiences that inform our judgments; settling on and interpreting correct moral standards; and deciding how to prioritize competing goods.

7   Rawls is one of the most well-known architects of the principle of reciprocity as it is used by contemporary liberal theorists. According to the principle or reciprocity as understood by Rawls, "our exercise of political power is proper only when we sincerely believe that the reasons we offer for our political action may reasonably be accepted by other citizens as a justification of those actions" (Introduction to *PL*, xlvi).

considered "beyond the pale" of liberal citizenship and need not be extended any special accommodation by lawmakers and citizens within the "pale."

If the liberal conception of respect is right, then it does seem to follow that arguments that depend for their validity on the acceptance of religious truths are inaccessible and therefore provide insufficient grounds for justifying law and public policy – at least where there is no equivalent argument available in purely "accessible" terms. Let us take religion here to include propositions that assume or assert the existence of God or the truth of a religious creed, or attribute some special, revelatory quality to Sacred Scripture or to some religious leader (e.g. papal infallibility).[8] All such arguments fail the accessibility test, since there are many intelligent people who accept the principle of reciprocity (and are thus reasonable) and for whom religious propositions of this kind would be foreign to their worldviews or incompatible with their present epistemic commitments. In light of this failure, liberals will argue not that the law should restrict citizens' freedom of expression, but that citizens ought to voluntarily abstain from publicly advocating laws or policies on the basis of religious or religion-dependent reasons.[9]

So far, we have described the argument for restraint from the point of view of liberal respect for persons. There is, however, also an argument that is often made from social stability concerns. What are the *consequences* or likely consequences of permitting, versus restricting, religious reasons within policy-oriented public discourse? Here, liberals like to put forward what Eberle has referred to as the "argument from Bosnia," which is essentially that the introduction of religious issues into public discourse is likely to generate acrimony and cycles of distrust and mutual hostility, and that it is even liable to provoke a new round of religious persecution. As Eberle points out, this argument derives much of its force from the destabilizing force that religion had in the seventeenth century wars of religion in Britain and Europe.[10]

The argument from stability goes something like this: in light of the devastating effect of mixing religion and politics during the wars of religion, and in

---

8   For definitions of religious reasons, see Perry, *Love and Power: The Role of Religion and Morality in American Politics*, 66–82; Audi, *Religious Commitment and Secular Reason*, 34–35; Greenawalt, *Private Consciences and Public Reasons*, 39; Weithman, *Religion and the Obligations of Citizenship*, 122.

9   We need not settle here *which* laws or which category of laws deserves special protection from religious grounding. Some, such as Audi, earmark significantly coercive laws for special treatment, while others, such as Rawls, earmark laws involving "constitutional essentials and basic justice."

10 For a comprehensive treatment and critique of the "argument from Bosnia" and of a more moderate form of this argument, see Christopher Eberle, *Religious Convictions in Liberal Politics* (Cambridge: Cambridge University Press, 2002), 152–86.

light of our own experiences of the acrimony, intolerance, and hostility aroused
by religious discourse, we ought to restrict it at least when it comes to serious
discussions about policy and law. The evil consequences averted by such a state
of affairs would easily outweigh any positive benefits that religious discourse
might bring to society. This sort of argument has been advanced by both Robert
Audi and Richard Rorty.[11]

Why liberal arguments for restraint fail

Let us consider the liberal arguments for restraint on their merits. First, consider the argument from stability. I believe this is the weaker argument, for two reasons: first, because I am skeptical that anyone can compile sufficient historical
and sociological evidence to prove the case either way, i.e. to prove that religious
discourse has generated more good than bad or more bad than good consequences overall. Second, liberals such as Audi who make the consequentialist
argument for restraint invariably fail to advert to the significant differences
between early modern Europe or present-day Bosnia, and present-day developed
liberal democratic cultures such as the United States and Western Europe. Even
if religious discourse was a force for repression and a force to be feared in early
modern Europe, the notion that religion poses similar threats in, say, Britain or
France or the United States in the year 2003 requires a special argument and
cannot be assumed as a given.[12]

The liberal argument from respect cannot be dispensed with quite so easily
as the argument from stability. Here, I will challenge the liberal argument on
two grounds: first, by way of a *reductio ad absurdum*, pointing out its absurd
logical consequences which seem to have escaped its proponents. Second, by
proposing a rival conception of respect that I believe is both more true-to-life
and compelling.

Let us begin with the *reductio ad absurdum*. Assuming an accessibility
requirement roughly along the lines sketched above, what sorts of reasons can
be accepted as legitimate grounds for advocating a policy or law? We have
already seen that religious reasons, broadly understood, are likely to fail the

---

11   See Audi, *Religious Commitment and Secular Reason*, 100–103; and Richard Rorty,
     "Defense of Minimalist Liberalism," in *Debating Democracy's Discontent*, eds.
     Anita L. Allen & Milton C. Regan, Jr. (Oxford: Oxford University Press, 1998).

12   This point is made forcefully by Eberle in *Religious Convictions in Liberal Politics*,
     158–66: "the argument from Bosnia founders on the fact that there are crucially
     important differences between the conditions that obtained in the confessional states
     party to the wars of religion. In particular, the confessional states' denial of religious
     freedom gave to religion an incendiary potential it lacks when citizens are free from
     the threat of persecution for their religious commitments and practices" (166).

accessibility test. But we have not yet considered what sorts of secular or non-religious reasons are likely to pass it. Recall that accessibility does not require *actual* acceptance of one's reason(s) for supporting a law, but rather, that the said reason must hook up in a plausible way with some aspect of the actual epistemic horizon of any "reasonable" citizen. It must be possible to embrace that reason without making some radical shift in one's belief system, without overcoming the burdens of judgment by overhauling one's worldview or radically revising one's moral commitments in life. One might even say that reasons offered for coercive laws should not be unduly epistemically challenging.

But this accessibility requirement is so demanding that it would immediately exclude a whole host of secular or non-religious reasons that seem to constitute the bread-and-butter of democratic deliberation. Here are a few sorts of reasons that I can think of that might be used as a basis for arguing for laws: the view that it is the responsibility of society to re-distribute wealth based on need rather than desert or performance; the view that human beings are morally inviolable at every stage of life; the view that the right to self-determination or autonomy trumps moral flourishing or well-being even to the point of justifying assisted suicide; the view that certain forms of art are worthy of state support and promotion more than, say, people's use of pornography. The list can be easily expanded, but the point to note here is that the set of legitimate laws as well as the set of legitimate contributions to public discourse must shrink considerably if the accessibility requirement is taken seriously, since none of the reasons I have just mentioned meets it. All of these reasons, and many others besides, fail to hook into the epistemic horizons of many actual reasonable people, i.e., in many cases, they could not be accepted without a radical shift in a person's worldview. As such, they violate liberal respect for a person's autonomy.

Can we seriously entertain the view that the legitimacy or acceptability of a public argument for a policy or law depends on its advocate's success in adducing grounds that are "accessible," in this strong Rawlsian sense, to all reasonable citizens? I think the consequences of this view are so absurd as to rule it out as a plausible interpretation of legitimacy. Wherever we find deep disagreement about the grounds for law we are likely to find disagreement based on parting worldviews or epistemic horizons. Should such a deep disagreement vitiate the legitimacy of the democratic outcome? Perhaps in some cases, yes. But not necessarily. This will become clearer, I hope, as I suggest an alternative conception of respect.

Faced with deep disagreement concerning the appropriate grounds of a law or public policy, what behavior best reflects genuine respect for my fellow citizen? The liberal answer goes something like this: seek some ground that both of you, *given your present (reasonable) epistemic horizons*, could potentially accept. But this concept of respect seems implausible to me, both because it rules out most attempts to justify laws and policies (as we have seen), and because it seems to assume an implausibly demanding view of autonomy. There is no good reason to think that just because my reasons for coercing another are presently inaccessible to that person in light of their accumulated habits, lifestyle, and beliefs, I thereby do that person a wrong or fail to respect her. Indeed, perhaps I do not even anticipate that the person will *ever* come round to accepting the grounds I offer. Instead of being bound by respect to offer shared reasons, I would suggest that I am bound by respect to offer reasons for coercion that are grounded in genuine interests of the coerced and of the society in question, and to give serious weight to the interest of a person in her own liberty or ability to shape her life in an individual and sometimes idiosyncratic way. Personal freedom and creativity can be quelled by an all-encompassing, heavily paternalistic state.

Of course, it may be objected that giving "serious weight" to considerations of personal liberty is altogether too vague a principle to guide legislators' and citizens' deliberations as they forge laws. However, this objection is almost certainly misplaced, arising out of a penchant for simplistic and "trumping" principles that is shared by many liberal theorists. The liberal conception of respect suffers from the simplistic absolutization of certain desiderata, most especially the desideratum of rational consent to coercive laws. While endeavoring to secure general consent to law, or at least as general a consent as can be secured, is a noble liberal goal, respect for citizens by no means *requires* universal consent to reasons for law as a matter of course.[13] There may be some extraordinary situations in which unanimous consent is morally required, but these do not concern us here. What concerns us here is how the central case of law is to be understood; what the conditions of legitimate coercion are in the most typical cases.

To recap, respect for persons does *not* require unanimous consent to coercive laws or universal accessibility of the grounds of such laws. It does require, however, that the proponents of such laws ground their arguments on the rational interests, broadly conceived,[14] of citizens and of the society at large, including the interest of citizens in their own liberty to shape their lives according to their individual purposes even if this means they may make mistakes from time to time.

---

13 Cf. Galston's and Raz's arguments that the violation of negative liberty in the interests of the individual affected cannot be considered wrong *in* principle (William Galston, *Liberal purposes: Goods, virtues and diversity in the liberal state* (Cambridge: Cambridge University Press, 1991), 86–87; Joseph Raz, *The Morality of Freedom* (Oxford: Clarendon Press, 1986), 157).

14 When I say, "rational interests," I do not mean interests conceived within a purely egoistic calculus or interests in some purely subjective sense. Nor do I suggest that the concept of "rational interest" can be completely separated from a person's subjective sense of well-being.

The Model of Public Discourse Behind the Principle of Restraint

The failure of arguments for religious restraint is rooted in a larger failure among liberals to develop a convincing account of the nature, dynamics, and goals of public discourse. Rawls, the paradigmatic Anglo-American liberal, conceives of discourse as a narrowly rationalistic, proposition-driven practice. This is also reflected in the work of Habermas, albeit under a somewhat different guise, as well as in the work of many recent liberal authors including Charles Larmore, Bruce Ackerman, Thomas Nagel, and Robert Audi.[15] According to this view, the theorist can helpfully focus in on those aspects of public discourse that consist of claims about how we ought to order our polity or what laws we ought to pass, and why. Essentially, public discourse consists of a set of normative or moral claims, along with more narrowly self-interested claims, which are justified publicly based on rational arguments that are assessed and accepted or rejected on their merits. This, at least, is the ideal picture offered by liberals. They do not deny that public discourse in reality contains many rhetorical and even manipulative appeals, but the pervasive assumption seems to be that we can best understand public discourse as a moral practice in terms of the interaction of equal and rational agents offering each other propositional arguments for policies and laws, arguments which are accepted or rejected on their merits. Call this the "propositional" model of public discourse. This liberal model of discourse is compatible either with the "constrained conversation" ideal of discourse advocated (under slightly different guises) by Ackerman, Larmore and Rawls, or with the comparatively "unconstrained" conversational ideal of Habermas and some deliberative democrats. I believe that both versions of the liberal conception of public discourse are seriously flawed. However, in this paper I will focus exclusively on the more constrained model.

According to the constrained-propositional model, when, in the course of a public discussion, we disagree on a coercive measure, we should bracket out our disagreement and proceed on the basis of what we share in common. Ackerman has a fairly simple version of this model, Rawls a more sophisticated one. But

---

15 See Jurgen Habermas, *The Theory of Communicative Action*, Vol. 1, trans. Thomas McCarthy (Boston: Beacon Press, 1984); and Jurgen Habermas, *The Theory of Communicative Action*, Vol. 2, trans. Thomas McCarthy (Boston: Beacon Press, 1987); Charles Larmore, "Political Liberalism," *Political Theory* 18, 3 (August 1990): 339–60; Bruce Ackerman, "Why Dialogue?" *Journal of Philosophy* 86, 1 (January 1989); Audi, *Religious Commitment and Secular Reason*; Nagel, "Moral Conflict and Political Legitimacy."

16 This idea is well-captured by Rawls's notion of finding an "overlapping consensus" upon which to build a conception of political justice. Similarly, it is expressed negatively by the "bracketing" strategy advocated by Ackerman to deal with fundamental moral conflict in political discourse (Ackerman, "Why Dialogue?," 16).

the central idea of proceeding on the basis of shared premises is common to both.[16] Of course, the liberal believes that this bracketing strategy will in fact enhance the legitimating and stabilizing functions of discourse. I, on the other hand, will argue that the liberal model of discourse, in this instance the con-strained-conversation model, is deeply inimical to both, and that this failure is due to the liberal's blindness to the rich complexity of discursive practices, whose significance can only be understood by moving beyond the realm of propositional arguments.[17]

Consider, first, the legitimating function of public discourse: a suitably structured public sphere (or spheres) of discourse is supposed to make it more likely that the laws of a polity be publicly justifiable to all or most of its citizens. But how are laws justified to citizens? Is it through a set of probative proposi-tions abstracted from particular worldviews? Sometimes, perhaps, but more often than not, it is either by appeal to one's interlocutor's particular belief-system – and this appeal can be propositional in form – or by appeal to the authority, knowledge, or expertise of this or that person. The legitimacy of laws is largely parasitic upon the legitimacy of the political system as a whole, and this in turn depends on a relationship of trust developing between rulers and the people. Bonds of trust go far further in reassuring people that (often complex) laws can be justified than propositional arguments. In short, the moral relation-ship and mutual trust expressed through public discourse between citizens, and between citizens and legislators, is often at least as important as rational argu-mentation in legitimating the democratic process. And this moral relationship depends on an attitude of respect and understanding far wider and deeper than the basic liberal conception of respect that we have alluded to previously.

Inherent in the legitimating function of discourse is its capacity to furnish us with *knowledge* and information relevant to the legitimacy, justice, and soundness of laws and policies. But, as several philosophers have argued (e.g. Thomas Kuhn, Hans Georg Gadamer, and Alasdair MacIntyre) new knowledge is not always acquired by working out implications of, or adding propositions to, an established stock of knowledge, but by confronting alternative conceptual frameworks in light of which one's established framework must be altered. If a Gadamerian "fusion of horizons" is a viable way of acquiring new knowledge, however, then any bracketing strategy – especially a relatively ambitious and unconditional one – has the potential to suppress new sources of knowledge and

---

17   For arguments against the liberal model of discourse and in favor of more complex and dynamic models, see, inter alia, Mark Kingwell, *A Civil Tongue: Justice, Dialogue, and the Politics of Pluralism* (University Park, Penn.: The Pennsylvania State University Press, 1995); Waldron, "Religious Contributions in Public Deliberation;" Hollenbach, "Contexts of the Political Role of Religion;" Iris Young, *Inclusion and Democracy* (Oxford: Oxford University Press, 2000); and Galston, *Liberal Purposes*, 98–117.

information. If citizens are not confronted with their differences in a fairly open and occasionally provocative way, they are deprived of opportunities to understand better the uniqueness and strengths and weaknesses of their own positions, and possibly adopt new beliefs that at first appeared foreign to them. Jeremy Waldron makes a compelling argument against the liberal bracketing strategy, appealing instead to a more dynamic conception.

> Even if people are exposed in argument to ideas over which they are bound to disagree – and how could any doctrine of public deliberation preclude that? – it does not follow that such exposure is pointless or oppressive. For one thing, it is important for people to be acquainted with the views that others hold. Even more important, however, is the possibility that my view may be improved, in its subtlety and depth, by exposure to a religion or a metaphysics that I am initially inclined to reject. . . .I mean to draw attention to an experience we all have had at one time or another, of having argued with someone whose world view was quite at odds with our own, and of having come away thinking, "I'm sure he's wrong, and I can't follow much of it, but still, it makes you think . . ." The prospect of losing that sort of effect in public discourse is, frankly, frightening – terrifying, even, if we are to imagine its being replaced by a form of "deliberation" that, in the name of "fairness" or "reasonableness" (or worse still, "balance") consists of bland appeals to harmless nostrums that are accepted without question on all sides. That is to imagine open-ended public debate reduced to the formal trivia of American television networks.[18]

Consider now the stabilizing function of public discourse: this is closely related to its legitimating function. Although it obviously involves the building of bonds of trust and mutual respect between citizens and between citizens and legislators, it also involves a willingness to abide by the laws of one's polity even when they strike one as misconceived or poorly thought out. It involves a sense of belonging and responsibility and ownership of one's nation. All of these can be fostered in important ways by a respectful and vigorous public discourse. In particular, public discourse fosters mutual understanding among citizens, and this in turn can sow the seeds of cooperation and mutual trust. None of this is merely a matter of propositional correctness or the justification of laws – it involves various modes of conduct and dispositions that occur within the discursive encounter.

What the foregoing remarks suggest is that any concern with justification of the law as a social practice rather than a merely theoretical endeavor, must take very seriously the wider social context and conditions for such a practice to flourish and succeed, and these conditions not only cannot be met by the propositional model; the propositional model actively frustrates them.

---

18   Waldron, "Religious Contributions in Public Deliberation," 841–42.

Shifting the Spotlight from Speech-Governing Rules to Action-Governing Virtues

Having considered some of the deficiencies of the propositional conception of public discourse, I would like to suggest that we re-think public discourse in more holistic and less narrowly rationalist and propositional terms. Public discourse is a space in which embodied human beings (not *merely* rational beings) encounter one another, relate to one another, endeavor to understand one another, and explore different ways of living together and of understanding their shared and individual lives. As an activity, public discourse involves flesh-and-blood human beings, and it is constituted by their more or less successful efforts to communicate with each other. Like all human practices, this is a practice that is subject to manipulation and abuse, but the student of discourse can develop an account that helps us identify ways in which discourse can fail or succeed from a moral and practical point of view. If we are to come to an adequate understanding of the legitimating, stabilizing, and epistemic or knowledge-enhancing functions of discourse and how best they can be realized, we must contend with the reality of discourse in a holistic rather than piecemeal fashion. Therefore, instead of focusing on the bare rational content of discourse – an approach which, as I have suggested, has proven extremely limited and not especially profitable – it is time to focus our attention on the moral habits, dispositions, and relationships that constitute public discourse. For convenience, I will refer to this as the *virtue-centered*, as opposed to the *rule-centered* or *propositional* conception of discourse. Here, I merely want to sketch some of the central elements of such an account; in the next section, I will consider some of its implications for the role of religion in public discourse.

In calling for a shift from content-oriented rules to action-oriented virtues in the study of public discourse, I am not of course suggesting that rules have no place at all in such an account. It is undoubtedly the case that given a certain understanding of appropriate and inappropriate, healthy and unhealthy, ways of relating to our fellow discussants, certain forms of discourse can be ruled out as disrespectful from the outset. However, what I am arguing against is the notion that whole categories of discourse, that we know can be potentially conducted in good faith and with the interests of society and individuals in view, can be ruled out of court as modes of assessing and justifying laws. This attempt at formulating ambitious principles of restraint to govern the content of discourse has proven impractical and self-defeating time and time again. It either results in trivial principles that almost all can agree to already, e.g., that nobody should publicly call for the indiscriminate imprisonment of this or that race, or it results in controversial principles that can only be justified by recourse to controversial worldviews, e.g., secularist epistemologies, which pre-emptively assume for themselves the epistemic function of discourse by pretending to settle complex normative and epistemological questions prior to the discursive engagement.

What, then, are the main elements of a virtue-centered account of discourse? They consist primarily of what I will call *communicative virtues*, virtues that one naturally associates with communication and especially with communication in a morally and culturally pluralistic polity. These virtues are not equivalent to Habermas' communicative ethics, which tends to treat discourse in a much more rationalist and propositional way. Some of the basic communicative virtues or moral excellences are the capacity to listen, the desire to understand one's interlocutor, truthfulness, magnanimity, humility, generosity, patience, perseverance, a genuine concern for the interests of one's neighbors, respect for personal freedom, tact, sensitivity and openness to the concerns and experiences of others, a willingness to back down when one is proven wrong, and a willingness to compromise within the bounds of moral integrity. As you can see, the list could be expanded quite easily. I believe a lot of energy has been wasted trying to work out hard-and-fast exclusionary rules to govern the content of discourse, when political philosophers' energies would be much more fruitfully expended exploring the content and implications of the communicative virtues.

One of the most promising virtue-centered accounts of discourse that I have encountered can be found in Mark Kingwell's *A Civil Tongue: Justice, Dialogue, and the Politics of Pluralism* (1995).[19] Kingwell claims that "just talk" is one of the central, if not *the* central, virtue of a just liberal society. Although he may exaggerate the importance and centrality of communication and discourse in a liberal democracy, there is no denying that today, perhaps more than ever before, the justice of a polity and the quality of its shared life are deeply dependent on the justice, fairness, and quality of its public discourse. Kingwell summarizes the virtues of discourse in the terms "politeness" and "civility," and suggests that these need not be conceived narrowly as the slavish pursuit of convention and etiquette, but as phonetic virtues that help a discussant adapt his or her behavior to any given discursive context. Although this requires a special kind of prudence, it is not merely tactical or strategic or narrowly self-interested or instrumental prudence. Rather, I would suggest that it is a prudence oriented towards the good of the other as well as one's own good and the good of one's polity, as these are realized through speech.

Perhaps one of the biggest selling-points of the virtue-centered account is that it is much more deferential towards the epistemic function of discourse, i.e., it recognizes that many difficult issues of epistemology and morality must be worked out through an open and honest discussion rather than settled prior to discussion by the "armchair theorist."[20] The virtue-centered account can accept

---

19 Mark Kingwell, *A Civil Tongue: Justice, Dialogue, and the Politics of Pluralism* (University Park, Penn.: The Pennsylvania State University Press, 1995). Thanks to Matt Mendham for bringing this book to my attention.

20 This is the thrust of Kingwell's criticism of proponents of what he calls "constrained

Waldron's dynamic, agonistic model of discourse outlined above and argue that only such an open-ended model can respect the epistemic function of discourse. Of course, the theorist has every right to share her ideas about social and political morality with the rest of the world, or with her academic colleagues, but she cannot pre-emptively settle heated moral disputes in advance of the discursive process. Rather than fixing the rules of discourse once and for all and in advance, she is joining her voice in an extended conversation. Of course, she may suggest that certain rules are desirable or undesirable, but many issues cannot be appropriately or realistically settled in advance of discourse itself. These include the appropriate political role, and the epistemic status, of religious propositions. Through discourse, this sort of issue can be gradually illuminated even if never settled definitively. This is part of the epistemic or knowledge-enhancing function of discourse. In short, the virtue-centered account does not establish rigid or comprehensive rules governing the content of discourse and thus tends to allow a lot more room for a Socratic quest for the truth among discussants, while structuring this quest with interpersonal dispositions and virtues that can be accepted as important by a very large proportion of thoughtful citizens.

Now, I would like to comment briefly on the advantages of a virtue-centered account for discourse's legitimating and stabilizing functions. First, by opening laws and policies to a wide range of challenges and interpretations, and permitting citizens to voice their interests and perspectives in a dynamic, give-and-take process, the virtue-centered account opens up the lawmaking process to a wider array of inputs and critical voices. This has two consequences for legitimacy: first, more citizens feel they can have some influence on the lawmaking process, and this enhances the democratic legitimacy of that process in their eyes and minimizes alienation and resentment towards political authority; second, the laws and policies are subjected to a wider-ranging critique and discussion, and insofar as criticisms are aired rather than artificially suppressed, lawmakers are made more publicly accountable and the legitimacy of laws is enhanced.

Now, the stabilizing function is closely allied to its legitimating function. The relationship can be captured roughly by saying that legitimacy or at least perceived legitimacy often has far-reaching consequences for the stability of a political regime, especially in a modern liberal democracy. Other things being equal, the greater the perceived legitimacy of a regime, the less likely that citizens will become disgruntled, rebellious, uncooperative, and violent. The virtue-centered account, by rejecting artificial theoretical restrictions on the

---

liberal dialogue": "instead of stopping short with a defensible clearing of dialogic space, and letting the citizens themselves decide what rules are just, Ackerman (like Rawls, Nozick, and others) wants to work out, in some detail, a set of justified rules" (Kingwell, *A Civil Tongue*, 51).

content of discourse, facilitates discursive outlets or channels for minority and majority views alike. Thus, views that more restrictive accounts would drive out of public discourse and into sub-cultures may be aired and tested in the to-and-fro of public discourse. This draws citizens into a shared or common public life, and thus fosters a sense of belonging and a sense that one is taken seriously by one's fellow citizens rather than dismissed out of hand. Bonds of mutual understanding and respect may develop in these circumstances if citizens exercise the interpersonal and communicative virtues required to make this process work well. It is only in the context of such an inclusive and civil conversation about the political common good that citizens can overcome their sense of alienation and mutual suspicion and develop a strong sense of loyalty to a common political enterprise, whether at the local or national level.

Re-assessing Religious Interventions in Public Discourse

In conclusion, I would like to consider some of the implications of the virtue-centered account for the role of religion in public discourse. Although this is not the place to embark on a comprehensive assessment of the question, a few of the more obvious points bear mentioning. First, a virtue-centered account, although rejecting in general the restraint-centered strategy and calling for a much more dynamic and agonistic model of discourse, does not issue a license to participants to bring up whatever they feel strongly about, whenever they feel like it, in whatever discursive context they find themselves in. On the contrary, it calls for an attitude of responsibility and a phonetic sensitivity to context among discussants. This means that intelligent discussants should recognize that discourse is a multi-faceted practice and that even a single person can assume different roles depending on the discursive context. How one behaves must be determined not only by the sum of one's convictions, but by the role one occupies (e.g., am I speaking as a son, a spouse, a colleague, a parent, a close friend, a fellow train passenger, a brother in faith, a legislator, a judge, a citizen, a campaigner?, etc.) and the particular person or group one is addressing (e.g., am I speaking to a person who is responsive to "tough talk" or somebody who is very sensitive and only requires gentle understatement in order to be responsive to my message?). Tact as well as legitimate strategic considerations often counsel that I exercise a sort of temperance in my speech and either remain silent or re-formulate my point in a manner that is will be more effective and constructive under the circumstances.

Although moral excellence in discourse can positively require deliberative restraint in certain contexts, there may well be other situations in which one finds that disagreement runs so deep and an issue is so pressing and important that the only realistic contribution one can hope to make is to witness to one's moral beliefs with courage and hope that at least some people will see the cogency of, be influenced by, or at least become aware of, one's position. This is a far cry from Ackerman's "constrained conversation"[21] or Rawls's notion of public reason, in which one is (morally) required to bracket one's comprehensive doctrines or deeply contentious views when talking about important political issues such as coercive law (for Ackerman) or fundamental justice (for Rawls).[22]

What does this tell us about the role of religion in public discourse? Well, it does not tell us that religion is *per se* an illegitimate basis for public argumentation about the law. Of course, neither does it suggest that any and every religiously-based argument for a law or policy is cogent, valid, or just. Rather, it suggests that religious discussants must determine themselves, moved by phonetic considerations and the communicative virtues as well as the contributions of other discussants, when restraint is and is not appropriate. At the limit, the legitimacy of their reliance on religion may be challenged by other discussants, but this challenge, if it is made in good faith rather than used as a trick to dismiss adversaries, may be met on its merits.

If religious believers exercise the virtues of communication, all of which I believe are consistent with most religions, then they will undoubtedly find that public discourse requires a strong moral character and a generous dose of fortitude and humility. However, they, along with those either opposed to or suspicious of religious discourse during policy discussions, will not need to flounder under any intellectually despotic or arbitrary exclusionary rules; instead, they should endeavor to understand rather than merely be understood; to listen rather than merely be heard; to address the concerns of others and not only their own concerns; and to allay the fears of others regarding the implications of religious discourse where this seems appropriate.

I do not claim that my account of discourse offers any neat resolution of the issues surrounding religious and moral diversity in liberal polities, nor do I think any realistic account could claim to offer such a resolution. However, I do believe that it offers a much more accurate description of the nature, dynamics, and goals of discourse than more traditional rule-centered models have offered, and I think it illuminates some important normative dimensions of discourse that most participants, religious and non-religious alike, can accept without compromising their deepest moral convictions. In short, it has the dual advantage of both being truer to the reality of public discourse as a social practice, and of offering a convincing basis for continuing the extended conversation about the common good in an atmosphere of freedom and mutual respect.

---

21 See Ackerman, "Why Dialogue?"

22 Rawls does allow the "proviso" that one may advance comprehensive reasons provided "public" reasons are advanced "in due course." But this proviso, apart from being quite vague (when is "in due course"?) still seems to require one to bracket comprehensive views if one does not anticipate an equivalent public reason emerging

ON JOHN RIST'S
REAL ETHICS

The Need for the Intellect in Moral Realism

Michael A. Dauphinais

Professor Rist has offered us an impressive book. Its expansive scope alone would be remarkable even if it were not for the fact that Rist has accomplished an unusual feat in contemporary philosophy – namely, doing philosophy within an historical tradition without falling into the opposite problem of relegating the tradition to the history of philosophy. The book thus draws heavily upon the inquiry of Plato, yet never as though the goal was the understanding of only the texts themselves, instead of the reality of man and God that the texts elucidate and point towards. The sustained analysis of Plato's thought, especially as expressed in the *Republic*, gives rise to an analysis of an impressive array of modern and contemporary moral philosophers, from Kant and Hume to Parfit and Rawls. I would express the overall thesis of the book in a two-fold manner: contemporary moral philosophy no longer possesses the metaphysical framework, and the corresponding objective moral realism, necessary to avoid the conclusions of Nietzsche (or Foucault or Thrasymachus); thus contemporary moral philosophy must be eschewed in favor of a Platonic moral realism that alone offers a coherent view of human life. The books does not proceed by means of a point-by-point rebuttal of such moral philosophers of liberalism, but rather by showing that their project fails in offering self-justification at the same point where the project of moral realism, above all as articulated by Plato, can defend itself. In this way, Rist's own book instantiates his argument about Plato's method of proceeding in the *Republic* – the only way to show convincingly the error of those who reject foundations with respect to the nature of justice is to depict the full socio-political consequences of a rejection of the objective moral demands of justice.

My response will focus on raising three questions. First, what is the status of justification of moral beliefs and might not Aristotle also offer a kind of justification in a non-Cartesian fashion? Second, does Aristotle really fail in the manner that modern philosophy will later fail – namely, separating ethics from metaphysics? Third, what is the relationship between God and the community as the dual antidotes to the divided moral self? All of these questions concern the need to depict the moral self properly as an intellectual agent capable of gazing at truth.

Rist offers an intriguing stance on the question of the justification of moral beliefs. He criticizes Aristotle for assuming too much, on the one hand (29), and Descartes for engaging in an "'epistemological' hunt for certainty" (79). He suggests that in Plato's *Republic*, Socrates does not answer the challenge posed by Glaucon and Adeimantus directly because no "strictly demonstrable conclusions" are possible (32). Instead, Socrates begins the elaborate description and analysis of an ideal *polis* that will disclose the reality of justice. If the true nature of justice – and why it is good in itself to be just and not merely to have the reputation of justice – can be seen through the city, then belief in moral realism will have been justified. Some external standard of Goodness (identified by Plato as the form of the Good and later by Augustine as the eternal God in whom all the forms subsist as identical with his divine nature) is necessary to respond to Thrasymachus' dismissal of justice as truly good and offering happiness/*eudaimonia*. As Rist helpfully delineates, the debate between Socrates and Thrasymachus is not between two differing views of happiness, but between a view of man ordered towards happiness and a view of man in which the very conception of happiness has been undermined. This allows us to raise the question about whether Plato's overall project here differs from Aristotle's as much as Rist suggests. It seems that both Plato and Aristotle (and Rist) hold that one cannot directly refute those who deny moral realism. In the *Republic*, Plato claims that the only adequate response comes through a large narrative describing the necessity of justice as well as the unfortunate outcomes without an objective standard of goodness.

The works of Aristotle from the *Metaphysics*, to the *de Anima*, to the *Nicomachean Ethics* when taken together likewise display a similarly grand narrative. From the prime mover, to the human intellect which can rise to universals on the basis of sense experience, to the man who by nature desires the good and can seek to practice virtue and contemplate the divine nature, Aristotle's philosophy displays a framework larger than ethics. The broader philosophic argument displays that man could not be conceived as ordered towards happiness apart from his specific human nature as well as the existence of the divine nature. Aristotle thus grounds his ethical claims in an understanding of metaphysics and anthropology. Rist is correct in saying that Aristotle deemphasizes the divine nature as good and denies the independent existence of the form of the good. Aristotle leaves the good as simply that under which all human beings desire. This does not indicate that it lacks metaphysical existence, but simply says that the objective good cannot be separated from our desire for it. This suggests an incomplete understanding of the divine nature, but it will later be completed by Augustine and Aquinas's understanding of God.

Aristotle's overall project, particularly expressed in his *Ethics*, can be seen to function with some similarities to the way of Plato's argument in the *Republic*. Rist rightly observes that Aristotle does not address the specific objections of those who deny the whole character of morality and justice. But Aristotle does presuppose the moral realism of Plato in his own writings on ethics and therefore also shows by implication that without an objective moral framework even the language of the virtues and vices would collapse. Virtue causes those who possess it to be good and to function well as human beings. In a true friendship, each friend desires the good of the other for the sake of the other. In the ultimate happiness of man in contemplating the prime mover, truth itself is known for its own sake. This characteristic seen at all three aspects of the ethical life in Aristotle – or as Augustine would later put it, love of self, love of neighbor, and love of God – is an extended narrative that man would cease to be ethical or moral if there were not some objective good that made possible such desires for the good beyond what is merely useful to an individual's self-interest. So this is my first question: Does not the overall project of Aristotle work in a similar manner of justifying a moral realism? I am aware that many contemporary rational-choice moral philosophers appeal back to aspects of practical rationality of Aristotle, but if one is willing to read Plato sympathetically and through the corrective of later Augustinianism, as Rist does so admirably, could not one do the same with Aristotle?

This brings us to the heart of Rist's hesitations about Aristotle's approach to morality. Rist deems Aristotle's view of human nature flawed since Aristotle considers man from a third-person perspective and therefore fails to do justice to the moral character of the human being. His emphasis on the unity of the body and soul is variously described as an ontological, scientific, or third-person view and this is contrasted with Plato's moral, dualistic, and first-person view of human nature. Rist criticizes Aristotle for taking the mind to be the definitive aspect of the human being, i.e., what separates us from other animals. For Rist, the emphasis on the intellect fails to appreciate the distinctiveness of the moral will. Aristotle thus hides the reality of moral obligation under the need for rationality. Rist himself elaborates on what Aristotle means by "the mind," saying it is "especially viewed in its deliberative capacity, its ability to derive means to ends." But one may ask whether this eschews the reality of moral obligation. The ability to derive means to ends comes at the heart of the moral life since the moral life surely must evaluate obligations and goods in light of our ability to derive means in concrete situations. One specific criticism of Aristotle offered by Rist is that Aristotle "has concentrated on man as a metaphysical unity rather than as a divided moral subject" (87). This seems to be a weak criticism, since if one objects that Aristotle's account of *akrasia* is inadequate, the lack of metaphysical unity is surely just as large of a problem for Plato. If man is not a metaphysical unity, then the very search for a unified ethical account becomes unintelligible.

The issue of divided moral selves shows that the theme of conversion is central to Rist's project and the preference for a Platonic approach to the moral life is that it gives a better account of conversion than does Aristotle. Augustine's *Confessions* certainly improves on both Aristotle and Plato, but I do not see how a sophisticated reading of Aristotle's *Ethics* precludes such conversions. Aristotle's comments to the contrary should be seen within his overall philosophical approach which begins by considering things working well before considering problems. For instance, Aristotle first considers sight perception in a well-functioning case before examining problems in perception such as why a pole appears to be bent when placed halfway into water. Thus for the question of the good life for man, Aristotle begins with one who is well-brought up and continues to acquire the virtues more deeply with each passing year. This does not mean that moral conversions do not happen, but that the best case scenario is the more important object of analysis. Rist himself indicates that Plotinus has to reach false conclusions about a core self in order to explain moral conversion. This indicates that apart from a Christian conception of God and grace, and even with such an explanation, the fact of conversion remains mysterious whether in a Platonic or an Aristotelian approach. My second question concerns this seeming unsympathetic reading of Aristotle and the apparent rejection of the intellectual component of the moral life. If the overall project is to justify moral realism by showing the implications of its rejections, why not present the strengths of Aristotle combined with the strengths of Plato? More specifically, does not the moral self of Plato require a sufficient account of the intellectual grasp of reality in order to achieve the moral realism sought by Rist?

Now I turn to Rist's attempt to argue for the necessity of God and the community in order for human beings to become less divided. Rist suggests a moral argument for the existence of God based on the fact of moral improvement (81). Since there is no core, non-empirical, self as Plato and Plotinus had suggested, God enables us to improve along Augustinian lines. In terms of the community, Rist argues later in the book that a divided self is in need of external correction and that this correction comes in the form of the human community that inculcates in us a moral sense of responsibility towards others (219). Moral responsibility cannot be mere habituation, but must come from without in a way that allows us to see that such responsibility is necessary for moral coherence. In these two ways, Rist has dealt a strong argument against the enlightened individualism of our age and made philosophical room for God and the Church as providing the necessary supports for human freedom. Apart from the external helps of God and the community, human beings lack the freedom to be moral, that is, the freedom to do the good, the freedom to become less divided in one's desires so that one's desires can be fulfilled in the possession of the true good. This brings me to my third question, what is the relationship between God and the human community. Both seem to function in a similar role of correcting our divided selves. How then, on Rist's account, is one not superfluous to the other? In other words, why cannot the contemporary anti-realist who sees the force of Rist's approach choose to embrace the human community apart from God? Does not the moral account of God as that which unites our divided moral selves need to be supported by an intellectual account of God as the cause of our very existence?

The fundamental unity to this response concerns the situation of Aristotelian metaphysics. I accept Rist's argument that most post-Enlightenment theories of morality fail when divorced from their grounding in the classical metaphysics that was taken up and transformed by Christian revelation. As we have seen, he indicates that the divorce of metaphysics and ethics begins with Aristotle and his overly intellectualistic approach to human nature. Although Rist avoids being hoisted on his own petard, nonetheless, the anti-intellectual thrust of his argument contains significant risks. How can an understanding of morality adequately rooted in metaphysical claims not include the intellect's gaze at reality associated with the Aristotelian tradition of philosophy? Platonism needed a peculiar set of metaphysical assumptions in order to make sense of the human person's knowing and loving objects both in, and transcending, our experience of the world. Aristotle's approach through his metaphysics, anthropology, and ethics grounded a moral realism without having to posit distinctly existing forms or complex accounts of learning as remembering. In the thirteenth century, Aquinas, for instance, drew heavily on both Aristotelian and neo-Platonic sources in his theological and philosophical inquiry. The Aristotelian emphasis on natures and their *teloi* combined with its account of the unmoved mover provided Aquinas with a means of rendering intelligible a world brought into being by a free Creator. The metaphysics and ethics are intertwined. Because we have been created by a self-subsisting Being of sheer act, we only find our true selves as we come to know and to love that one whom we call God. This is not to say at all that Aristotle's approach is complete in itself or that the neo-Platonic conception of Being and beings, and the corresponding and rich understanding of participation, is already present in Aristotle. The point is simply that if Rist sustains his anti-Aristotelian stance, specifically on the grounds of Rist's reaction against intellectualistic accounts of human nature, it remains unclear whether his emphasis on the moral self alone can provide the metaphysical grounding he rightly recognizes is absent in contemporary moral philosophy.

The Upward Journey of the Soul

Daniel McInerny

Any defense of Moral Realism.must include an account of those "strange pris-oners"[1] which Plato has his Socrates describe as dwelling at the bottom of a cave, their necks and legs fettered, who are only able to see themselves, or any-thing else, as shadows cast against the wall in front of them, and who mistake those shadows for reality.

Any defense of moral realism, that is, demands an account, not only of what is real, but of how we are deceived by appearances of reality, deceived either by ourselves, by others, or by some combination of the two (I say "we," for, as Plato says, these strange prisoners at the bottom of the cave are, in fact, "like us").[2] But a defense of moral realism also demands a narrative of our liberation from such deception, what Socrates calls "the upward journey of the soul to the intel-ligible realm" (517b). This will be an account of how, by education of all sorts, we can be led, stumbling, out of the cave of ignorance and bad habit and into the light of knowledge and virtue.

In the trenchant and eminently enjoyable defense of moral realism that we find in John M. Rist's *Real Ethics*, both sorts of account arc madc available, and the challenges they propose for mainstream academic moral philosophy – not to mention moral theology – are formidable. Those challenges might be summed up most neatly in the form of an opposition: not so much one between Nietzsche and Aristotle, but rather between all those modern and contemporary ethical theories that either explicitly aver or devolve into the affirmation of autonomous human choice, on the one hand, and, on the other, what Professor Rist calls a "Christianized system of Platonic realism" (139). In more marketable terms, contemporary ethics comes down to the question of "Nietzsche or Augustine?"

---

1 Translations from the *Republic* are taken from G. M. A. Grube's translation, revised by C. D. C. Reeve, found in John M. Cooper, ed., *Plato: Complete Works* (Indianapolis, IN: Hackett Publishing Company, 1997).

2 Alasdair MacIntyre has recently stressed the importance for natural law theorists, for example, to provide with their accounts a "theory of error." See his "Theories of Natural Law in the Culture of Advanced Modernity," in Edward B. McLean, ed., *Common Truths: New Perspectives on Natural Law* (Wilmington, DE: ISI Books, 2000), pp. 91–115.

The aspect of Professor Rist's argument that I would like to focus on in this comment is what I just referred to as the narrative of liberation from moral deception. I want to explore, in other words, how in Professor Rist's account moral conversion and progression is possible. How do we move from appearance to reality?

Something must first be said, however, about what it means to be locked into the world of appearances. Given the Platonic influence upon Professor Rist's argument, it is not unfitting to pursue this task by way of a few, brief modifications on the allegory of the cave.

As with Plato, what for Professor Rist binds the strange prisoners at the bottom of the cave is ignorance, mistaken notions, and bad habit. In their – our – moral bondage, the prisoners gaze at shadows, but principally shadows of themselves. How many, and of what character, are the shadow selves they see? There at least three of them, embodied in three possible types of life: first, there is "a life in which our reasoned love of virtue governs our possessiveness;" second, "a life directed by a love of honor, status and self-respect;" and third, "a life of a Humean sort in which reason is (and *ought* only to be) the slave of the passions" (101).

These shadow selves are cast upon the wall by puppets paraded in front of a dying fire. The puppets correspond to the three types of life, informed mainly by caricature notions of the being and nature of God, of human nature, and of the human good – though some of them are informed by more genuine versions of these ideas. The dying light refers to the enlightened human intellect, emancipated from all extrinsic authority, especially from the authority of God's eternal law.

The chief ill effect of their bondage is that the prisoners are unable even to know themselves adequately, and so they tend to confuse themselves with the shadow selves they see on the wall. Since the shadows are many, a prisoner has a difficult time conceiving himself and his interests as a unity. He understands his life as a series of "lives," of compartmentalized roles. In Plato's version of this allegory, the prisoners while away the time by competing in silly contests: betting on which puppet will follow which, and the like. Applied to Professor Rist's argument, the game the prisoners play is the highly destructive power-play of radical choice between alternative, and often conflicting, shadow selves.

We thus begin to see that the turning point of any prisoner's life, the being unbound and led out of the cave, corresponds to a moral conversion in which the prisoner begins to move from an existence flitting between the divided lives of his various shadow selves, toward a greater and greater unity of self-understanding. As Professor Rist provocatively puts it, moral conversion is the beginning of a progression from a self, or from our various divided selves, toward a soul – understanding "soul" as the perfection and hence unification of all human powers; the state in which, as Plato puts it, each one of our capabilities "minds its own business," and we finally live one life (106).

The key to moral conversion and progression is self-reflection. More precisely, it is reflection upon the disharmony between the first- and second-order desires pursued by our shadow selves; upon, for example, the disharmony between our unchaste desires and our desire not to be unchaste – if only sometime, as with Augustine, in the future. Without this ability of self-reflection there would be no possibility of unity; we would be mere heaps rather than bundles of shadow selves that at least have the capability of being unified (106).

The picture here is of a set of second-order desires that serve as the measure of correction for our first-order desires. But what is the "ground" of correct second-order desires, and how do we discover it?

Professor Rist is adamant that the measure of our first-order desires must be something extrinsic to any and all of our various shadow selves. The appropriate ground of second-order desires is outside of us. Which is to say, moral improvement is not something that can be explained entirely or even principally by our own efforts. He sets up the issue as a *modus tollens* argument: If the moral improvement that human beings manifestly achieve is to be explained by our own efforts, then there must be some inner core to our humanity, untouched by sin. But since there is no such identifiable pure and inner core, then the moral improvement that human beings manifestly achieve cannot be explained by our own efforts (81). Professor Rist puts this forward as a moral argument for the existence of God.

All rides, however, on the claim that human beings fail to possess an inner core of humanity, untouched by sin, which sits underneath a casing of ignorance, mistaken belief, and bad habit like a pearl in the middle of an oyster. Clearly, there is no point in disputing that human behavior is fundamentally infected by what Professor Rist calls the "surd-factor," a radical source of division between human desires that makes possible the variety of our shadow shelves (71). And clearly, any good Christian or even pagan view should understand that only in the desire for God as our highest good, a good that subsumes, not merely replaces, other goods, can the conflicts of human nature be brought into any semblance of harmony.

But Professor Rist's argument goes farther. He argues that what is wanted for moral conversion and progression is more than a Platonic-style *eros* for the Good, but a purified erotic love for God consisting in a friendship initiated by God Himself (109-110). Why this must be so is twofold. First, because in order to show love one must first be able to receive it (implying that our successful love for God is dependent upon our ability to receive it from Him); and second, following from this, because we can only receive love from God if we conceive Him as a personal entity with whom we can enter into friendship. Professor Rist concludes, "Clearly it would not be possible for any striving of ours to achieve such a friendship; it would require not only God's turning to us, but his turning as a friend – which seems to be explicable only in terms of the Pauline theology of *kenosis*, of the condescension of God to our created level, enabling us to return, by a purified *eros*, to himself" (110).

Successful moral conversion and progression, then, to what extent it is achievable in this life, is only possible on the level of the theological virtues – a conclusion that is unimpeachable from the standpoint of supernatural truth, but one that leaves the non-believer, or even the Christian concerned with philosophical arguments, wondering what place there is in this narrative of liberation for the *natural* knowledge of the human good.

Professor Rist's thoughts on this question come to the fore in his discussion of Thomistic natural law theory. Here he tenaciously and rightly takes exception to the recent reconstruction of Thomistic natural law theory by Anthony Lisska, which argues that Aquinas's theory "can be defended – and was intended to be defended – without reference to the existence of God" (152). But in doing so he makes three distinctions the effect of which is to bring out of focus the significance of our natural knowledge of the human good.

The first distinction is that between the natural law and God's eternal law. The reason why the attempt to depict Thomistic natural law theory without its theistic dimension is futile, according to Professor Rist, is because it neglects the very definition of the natural law given by Aquinas: the natural law is, by definition, the rational creature's participation in God's eternal law (152, quoting *ST*, I II, q. 91, a. 2). This much, of course, is true. But when it comes to the issue of moral conversion and progression, to helping someone out of the cave, one does not start with a view of the natural law in the order of being. What one needs is to locate some basic and shared truths that not even a lifelong prisoner to modern moral philosophy could dispute. The task is to highlight truths about the human good already accepted by the prisoner via what Aquinas calls his *inclinationes* (*ST*, I-II, q. 94, a. 2). These naturally known truths are very general, to be sure, and will often be obscured by ignorance, mistaken belief, and bad habit, but except in instances of grave depravity they remain available to all human agents, and so serve as the beginnings, *already in us* (not just in the future), of what Professor Rist calls our "soul," our fully-perfected and unified moral self.

There is no question here of taking God out of the picture, and this in two ways. First of all, and again, the precepts governing the *inclinationes* of our nature are, in the order of being, the precepts of God's eternal law. But even in the order of discovery of moral truth, with which I am interested here, the *inclinationes* exist in an order that tracks the hierarchical order of goods culminating in the *summum bonum* that is God (*ST*, I-II, q. 94, a. 2). Our first and most important inclination, in other words, is for a good that will fully satisfy our desire for goodness, for finality and self-sufficiency, for unity. This is not to say that all, or even most, will, apart from revelation and good education, identify the *summmum bonum* with anything so edifying as Aristotle's God. But it is to say that in the desire for ultimate goodness, in the recognition of our duty to pursue truth, and above all truth about the highest things, we have the starting-point for serious philosophical reflection about the nature of the *summum bonum*, the kind of dialectical reflection masterfully pursued by Aquinas in questions 2 and 3 of the *Prima secundae*. Without such a starting-point, there is simply no place for philosophical reflection, at least, to begin.

I take it, however, not that Professor Rist would disagree with what I am saying, but that he would argue that in underscoring our initial knowledge of our natural end I am talking about what is only, in our post-lapsarian state, "a creation of analysis, not a phenomenon of human life" (153). Here he marks a second distinction, that between man's imperfect and perfect happiness. "Roughly speaking," he writes, "according to Aquinas, natural happiness, that is, the perfection of man's powers [. . .] is Aristotle's goal; while perfect happiness is that perfection of man's potentialities (not only of his original capabilities) which would raise him to the company of the blessed and is only available through the sacrifice of Christ and man's adoption by God" (152). Professor Rist is right to remark that one cannot approach the secularist by arguing that natural happiness "is an actual and present [. . .] possibility for man," and that perfect happiness "is added on to it rather than informing it" (153). In our *de facto* state, he concludes, our overriding end is supernatural, one that subsumes all natural goods into it, and thus it is misleading to approach Aquinas's natural law theory with any other understanding.

In his reading of Aquinas on this issue Professor Rist depends upon Benedict Ashley's article, "What is the End of the Human Person? The Vision of God and Integral Human Fulfillment," but I believe he has missed one of the key conclusions of Fr. Ashley's argument. In criticizing H. De Lubac's rejection of a natural end for human beings, Fr. Ashley remarks that such a position leads "to what for an Aristotelian, at least, is an absurdity – a human nature that is not a nature."[3] For if nature is defined as an intrinsic principle of motion and rest, and motion implies a pre-determined goal, then a nature without a final cause is impossible.[4] Thus Fr. Ashley concludes that "the human person even in our existential order has a natural finality which is ultimate in its own order, although God has graciously subordinated this finality to an infinitely higher supernatural one, so that while natural human fulfillment remains truly ultimate in its own natural order [. . .] it is only *relatively* ultimate."[5] Professor Rist does recognize the Thomistic point that man can only have two ultimate ends, a natural and a

---

3   B. Ashley, "What is the End of the Human Person? The Vision of God and Integral Human Fulfillment," in L. Gormally, ed., *Moral Truth and Moral Tradition: Essays in Honor of Peter Geach and Elizabeth Anscombe* (Dublin: Four Courts, 1994), 80.
4   Ibid.
5   Ibid, 81.

supernatural, if one is ordered to the other (153). But, *contra* Fr. Ashley, he chooses not to emphasize the ultimacy of our natural end within the natural order, and the importance that ultimacy has for theistic, philosophical reflection. My contention is that the understanding of this ultimacy is the starting-point, the *theistic* starting point, both for the moral conversion of those who do not share the Christian faith and for the philosophical justification of God as the point and purpose of human action.

A third and final distinction Professor Rist makes impacting our natural knowledge of the human good is that between being guided by prudence and being under an obligation in law. "If we are a substantial set of dispositional properties tending to a certain end or good," Professor Rist writes, "there seem in a non-theistic naturalism to be no more than prudential arguments as to why the human race should accept that good. We incidentally may not want to be 'human' or 'fully human' in the sense towards which we are pointed. [. . .] Of course," he adds, "if we are designed by God to go in a certain direction as towards our ultimate and individual end, and if that directedness is the plan of an ultimate goodness, the situation is quite other" (155). Insofar as we are designed by and for God, in sum, human beings are to conceive of themselves as under obligation to the good; otherwise, to pursue one's flourishing is only to follow prudential judgment. My question is whether it makes for a sufficient understanding of obligation to recognize, in Aristotelian fashion, the ordered hierarchy of the human good governed – as Professor Rist understands Aristotle – by God as a final cause. Or does obligation require a notion of a loving law-giver who personally utters His commands? If the latter is the case, and if, as Professor Rist also says, "the element of inspiration to do right comes from whatever capacity we have to be motivated by the good (262)," then it is a puzzle why the Aristotelian picture of the good, based upon our natural knowledge, is insufficient to ground a theory of obligation.

In this comment I have been pointing toward the need for a rather robust theistic naturalism, one necessary to reflect philosophically about how moral conversion and progression toward unity can both occur and be justified. As I read Professor Rist's book, the emphasis of his argument is upon the need for a supernatural theism if we are going to get ourselves out of the cave. To be sure, this is true from the point of view of our supernatural end. But, taking my cue again from Fr. Ashley, if the grace requisite to achieve that supernatural end is to perfect, rather than supplant, human nature, then the integrity of the natural end for human beings, relative to its own order, must be upheld. The upward journey towards God demands that we must already be in possession, albeit imperfectly, of our souls.

Assessing and Strengthening the Metaphysics behind the Ethics

Barry A. David

In *Real Ethics*, John Rist at one point summarizes his argument by stating that a "realist theory of moral foundations . . . is unashamedly theological or at least metaphysical, being the more or less expanded metaphysical claim of Plato that there exists some eternal principle of goodness and intelligibility independent of the human mind."[1] Elsewhere, he writes that "realist" philosophers require the right attitude towards *tradition* to meet today's challenges and advance our understanding of ethics.[2] If we set together these two claims, it seems appropriate to consider the place of Rist's book within "the tradition" and analyze his use of divine principle.

This is worth studying for two reasons. First, if ethics must be grounded in a "reformed" Platonic metaphysics, and "a better knowledge of God brings a better knowledge of man,"[3] then a more precise knowledge of the divine principle in which man participates will provide us with a more exact foundation. Second, even though Rist has only intended to elucidate *the minimum requirements* of a realist ethics and has relied, for this reason, upon decisive aspects of Augustine's doctrines of God and man,[4] it is surely the responsibility of the realist philosopher (as Rist portrays him) to justify philosophically the nature of the Good in which his teaching is grounded. Adherence to a strict realist methodology[5] – *which is absolutely inseparable from any Platonic conception of God and*

---

1   J.M. Rist, *Real Ethics; Reconsidering the Foundations of Morality* (New York: Cambridge University Press, 2002), 271.
2   *Ibid.*, 278: "Thus a tradition needs not only to be a repository of the past wisdom of its society, but to be for ever able to update the expression of that wisdom in different historical contexts, enriching our understanding of it in the face of continually new and unexpected challenges."
3   *Ibid.*, 261: "And inadequate accounts of God, as I have [. . .] observed, supply or support correspondingly inadequate accounts of man."
4   *Ibid.*, 45.
5   By this I include "reformed" (i.e. Christian-Platonist) doctrines of God, substance, downward participation (viz. that created substances exist by participation in God),

Man – demands that we try to know the Good in which man participates. As Plato remarks in *Republic* 6: "the Form of the Good is the greatest object of study, and . . . it is by their relation to it that just actions and the other things become useful and beneficial. . . . If we do not know [the Good] even the fullest possible knowledge of other things is no help to us."[6] So by this standard, Rist's argument will be strengthened if we can identify and justify the divine principle in which it is anchored.

By analyzing Rist's doctrine of God, I will argue that a coherent theistic ethic needs to be explicitly anchored in a divine principle that (i) is concretely united with man (i.e. with human substance, soul and body), and (ii) "contains" non-participated eternal "relations" consisting in its eternally "causing" itself[7], knowing itself, and loving itself. This is because that conception of the divine – which approximates the Christian-Platonist doctrines of divine incarnation and Trinity – will necessarily mandate ethical teaching that (i) includes a cogent doctrine of human motivation, (ii) and (by striving to unify "the whole man with the whole God') avoids the incomplete accounts of human nature and action that will ultimately characterize both lesser instances of theistic ethics and all avowedly secular ethical systems. In light of the inspiration behind this conference, I will finish by showing how Thomas" teaching on law is a theistic ethic exemplifying these principles.

Rist grounds his defense of realist ethics in Augustinian accounts of God and Man since ". . . historically speaking, the essentials of any possible realist metaphysic are now securely in place: there is no immediate need to pursue further refinements."[8] This is not only because Augustine corrects, develops, and supercedes that which is found in his (pagan and Christian) Platonist inheritance

---

upward participation (viz. that man is created in relationship with and to achieve union with God), mind (viz. that man is governed by his reason which is structured by three co-implicate powers co-extensive with mind itself – awareness/memory [or being/existence], understanding, and love/willing), and evil as privation. I include arguments as apparently diverse as Plato's *Line*, Aristotle's *Metaphysics*, Augustine's *de Trinitate* (*Trin.*), Anselm's *Proslogion*, and each of Aquinas's 'five ways' and his *Summa Theologica* itself.

6   *The Republic*, trans. G.M.A. Grube (Indianapolis: Hackett Publishing Company, 1974), 6, 505a, 159–160.

7   When I say that the divine "causes itself" I use the term "cause" analogously and mean *the sort of thing*, viz. eternal generation, that Plotinus describes in *ennead* 5.1.6 and Christians signify by the divine "begetting" and "proceeding" when explaining the divine processions. I do not mean that the eternal, incorruptible, and incorporeal divine substance brings itself into being or undergoes temporal change. For a corrected Platonic view of the divine life see Augustine's argument in *Trin.* 5–15.

8   Rist, 45.

but also because his "adaptation of Platonic metaphysics . . . has dominated all subsequent Christian philosophy in the West, including, at relevant foundational points, that of the Thomist."[9] On this basis, Augustine is described as "the father-in-chief of the most cogently corrected form of the "Platonic" tradition."[10]

To support my belief that a richer metaphysics would strengthen Rist's presentation, I will analyze principally his concept of "God" since this grounds his philosophical psychology.[11] Rist selects Augustine's God because He includes what is best in Plato's Good and gods, Aristotle's God, the Jewish concept of God – and more. Augustine's God is personal, lovable, the standard and exemplar of moral goodness, self-knowing, the first efficient cause, omnipotent, providential, lawgiver, and "active promoter of moral goodness."[12] By the end of his essay, Rist has focused his theology to the point that what must be emphasized, above all else, are the attributes of power/creator, truth, and love (identified with God's Holy Spirit[13]) both (i) above all other attributes and (ii) (apparently) as equal between themselves. Without maintaining these two conditions we are beset by several awkward consequences – both practical and speculative – that I will now develop.

These awkward consequences are essentially threefold. (1) To begin with, it is unrealistic to maintain we would obey God's law "because He is omnipotent and will punish us if we act otherwise" for this would contradict our inclinations (defective though they may be) to understand and to love. Since *we are neither completely irrational nor completely incapable of right love, a relationship motivated by fear and blind obedience is unsatisfactory.* Under these circumstances God would have the appearance of an arbitrary, irrational, and selfish tyrant – and, under "normal" conditions, who would want to obey that kind of person? Hence, we need to understand God *not only* as power – for in certain contexts "the fear of the Lord" can usefully counter our irrational and self-destructive tendencies[14] – but also as truth and love if we will have the motivation to obey.[15] To hold otherwise denies a coherent account (i) of God as truth and goodness/love and (ii) of the mind's inclinations to knowledge and love of good.

---

9   *Ibid.*, 38.
10   *Ibid.*, 106.
11   For the reason mentioned above and because of the time constraints on this presentation, I will not focus directly on Rist's philosophical psychology/Augustinian concept of man.
12   Rist, 42.
13   *Ibid.*, 106.
14   I think here of Rist's Augustinian assertion (71, 263) that man is beset by a surd-factor *a.k.a.* the twin difficulties of ignorance and concupiscence.
15   Rist writes (261–2): "But if God's other attributes are swallowed up by the emphasis on his power . . . then to say that what we are commanded is right is no more than to say that the power disposed by God is right. That, as I have allowed, seems to

(2) Likewise, it is unrealistic to hold that we obey God's law simply "because His commands make rational sense" since – insofar as we are beset by the "surd-factor," i.e. by ignorance and concupiscence – *we are not completely rational.* To obey God since "He is truth" will satisfy our inclinations for intelligibility and love of goodness but, taken in isolation, it will fail to address our own unreasonableness, endemic ignorance, and tendencies towards self-destruction and deception. Accordingly, we need to understand God not only as truth but also as power and goodness/love if we will have motivation to obey. Otherwise we contradict coherent accounts of God and of the primary inclinations (and deficiencies) structuring the mind.

(3) Finally, it is equally unrealistic to maintain that a doctrine identifying God, above all else, as love will provide sufficient motivation for human obedience since – insofar as we seek intelligibility and are beset by the surd-factor – our love is unstable and very often wrongly ordered. To obey God because He is love will satisfy our inclination to love what is good and need for divine grace to achieve permanent integration. But taken in isolation from the attributes considered above, it would fail to address our inclination for intelligibility on the one hand (i.e. the need to perceive God as truth) and our tendency towards self-destructive love (and therefore our need to perceive God as power)[16] on the other hand. Although circumstances may often arise where we emphasize, to a greater degree, one or a couple of the aforementioned aspects of God we need, in the long run, to view Him not only as goodness/love but also as truth and power if we will have the right motivation to obey.

As I see it, the realist philosopher who thinks otherwise introduces two undesirable effects. First, he makes problematic human obedience since the structure of the mind and, therefore, the nature of motivation would be ignored. Correspondingly, he denies a satisfactory notion of God. If we maintain that God is only and/or primarily power or truth or love/goodness, we imply either (i) that He is without certain perfections we perceive in the created order or (ii) that the perfections we recognize are arranged in Him hierarchically – in the

---

point towards a "morality" of obedience hard to justify as morality at all. If, however, God's love is an attribute inseparable from his power, we can be certain that what he commands will not be right *merely* because he commands it . . . but right because it is good as God is good. There are two possible forms of "divine command morality', only one of which – that which assumes the loving goodness of God – is compatible with our sense that if something be right it is not right merely because it is the will of a superior."

16   Yet Rist also maintains (275) that in certain contexts it is fitting to emphasize divine power, fear of God and obedience – because of "the soul's weakened and divided state." He writes (*ibid.*): "This is where divine command moralities have their appeal, since fear may offer support where love and inspiration cannot, or cannot yet."

same way, perhaps, as Aristotle arranges the virtues in the virtuous man. In either instance, this could not be God of whom we speak. So, if we will have an adequate notion of God we need, at minimum, to accept the traditional doctrine (famously stated by Thomas) that since "the maximum in any genus is the cause of all that belongs to that genus" ". . . there must...be something which is to all beings the cause of their being, goodness, and every other perfection; and this we call God."[17] Hence, the perfections of power, love/goodness, and truth we find participated in the created order, and within which man requires a greater participation to achieve unity with God, are one and the same as the divine substance itself.

This doctrine of the divine simplicity (or of God as "the good of goods") is advantageous insofar as it allows us to (i) locate the aforementioned attributes in God and (ii) balance them equally with each other. But we might wonder how is it established that these are *the primary* attributes in God? There are other perfections besides these (e.g. beauty, nobility, justice etc. . . .), and why should they not also be emphasized? Perhaps power, truth, and love are emphasized because of the structure and requirements of the human mind. From where, then, does *this correspondence between the mind and those aspects of the divine* arise? Also, since we tend to order ourselves insufficiently due to the limitations of human reasoning, our endemic tendency to anthropomorphize, and our usually disproportionate relationship (brought about by ignorance and/or sin) towards one or another of the aforementioned attributes, how do we guard the aforesaid theology? A doctrine of the radical simplicity of divine substance will certainly support our emphasis on God's power, truth, and love, but there does not seem to be a necessary connection between the one teaching and the other. As a result, we will require a more complete account of God to support Rist's argument.

Lady Philosophy can help us here since according to a "reformed" principle of participation – i.e. a doctrine including the principles that "the being of lower *substances* depends on the being of higher and the highest substance" and "our ability to know the lower depends on our awareness/recognition of the higher and highest" – the divine principle must (i) be concretely united with man, and (ii) include supreme "inclinations" or "relations," so to speak, in which participate the primary human inclinations to God, viz. to His power/being, truth, and love/goodness. In the first instance, it is the clear implication of Platonic doctrine that mind's awareness of its privative relationship with God is presupposed by its awareness of its proper union with God and, therefore, of the existence of some exemplar union of God and man in which its very own thought and being participates.[18] If *the imperfect presupposes the perfect*,[19] if mind governs human substance, and if mind is aware of its incomplete

---

17   *S.T. I.* 2.3, *respondeo.*

union with God, then (i) the divine principle must be united with man, and (ii) there must be a way for him to achieve union with God, i.e. a doctrine of upward participation.[20] *Whether they recognize it or not*, it is ultimately on the basis of this account of the divine (and human) that Platonists in general and Rist in particular maintain that a "better knowledge of God brings a better knowledge of man." Otherwise we deny – or fail to develop adequately – the foundational realist doctrines of God, substance, participation, mind, and evil as privation.

We employ a similar logic to locate and characterize what I have named "the divine inclinations" or "relations." If mind participates *as image* in the divine – i.e. if mind, *as realists have always held*, is more like God than anything else – and if the primary inclinations structuring mind are ordered towards *existence (to be in the highest degree), truth (to know), and love (to will)*;[21] then these inclinations must stand as participations in some non-participated "relations" of being, truth, and love structuring the divine. I am not claiming to provide proof that God is Trinity – though I suppose I am moving in that direction. Rather, my point is that if what realists call "the inner man" participates more exactly in God than anything else, then what structures the "inner man" must participate more exactly in the divine life and reveal its character more than anything else. My procedure here, therefore, is more like Aristotle's in *Metaphysics 12* and Plotinus" in *Enneads 5-6* (i.e. analogical) than like Augustine's in *de Trinitate*, for it is one thing to show (by analogy from creatures) that God's life

---

18 We infer (by applying rigorously Platonic principles and concepts) not just the union of mind and/or soul with God but the union thereto of the whole human substance because – *maintaining rigorously the doctrine of substance* – the mind that knows God is found in the soul which is the substantial form of the human substance (composed of soul and body).

19 As Boethius writes: "It follows that if something is found to be imperfect in its kind, there must necessarily be something of that same kind which is perfect. For without a standard of perfection we cannot judge anything to be imperfect." (*The Consolation of Philosophy*, trans. R. Green, [Indianapolis: Bobbs-Merrill, 1962], book 3, prose 10, p. 61.)

20 This is part of the presupposition beneath Augustine's *Confessions*, viz. Christ, the perfect union of God and man. For as beautiful things presuppose Beauty itself, viz. God, and existing things presuppose Existence/Being itself, viz. God, so Augustine's awareness of his imperfect relationship with God presupposes some perfect relationship between God and man, viz. Christ, in which his own relationship with God participates. A similar logic lies beneath Augustine's analysis of the two cities in *de civitate Dei* and of the divine trinity in *Trin.*

21 I am relying here on something that is more like Augustine's paradigm in *conf.* 13.11.12 of being (*esse*), knowing (*nosse*), and willing (*uelle*) (for which he is indebted, to some extent, to Porphyry and Marius Victorinus) rather than on his further developed paradigm in *Trin.* 10–15 of memory/awareness (*memoria*), understanding (*intelligentia*), and willing (*voluntas/amor*).

has an ontological structure like that of the mind but quite another to provide persuasive evidence (by analogy from God Himself) that His life is Trinity since the structure of mind is trinitarian.[22] Nevertheless, despite the limitations of my procedure, it is clear that what is presupposed by Rist's Platonism – and, for that matter, by all realists – is a divine principle structured by eternal relations characterized by being, truth, and goodness/love. The immutable and self-complete divine substance, we might say, "eternally" "causes,"[23] knows, and loves itself; it causes itself knowing and loving itself; it knows itself causing and loving itself; and loves itself knowing and causing itself. In short, God must be self-knowing, self-loving, and self-causing. A contrary conclusion is tantamount to denying, amongst other things, that God is Reason.[24]

We learn two things from all this: first, that Rist's account of God is grounded in a coherent philosophical logic; and second, that a more rigorous application of that logic provides us with a more intelligible and persuasive account of theistic ethics. In the former regard, one benefit of the doctrine of divine simplicity is that the "whole man" must be included in sound ethical doctrine. If the universe consists in an array of substances participating to greater and lesser degrees in God, and the human person requires upward participation to achieve his proper end, then realist ethics must consider the unification with God not just of the soul or some part thereof but, instead, of the whole soul (reason, will, the emotions etc. . . .) and, therefore, body to which it is joined. Or, put differently, if ethicists do not view man in light of a right understanding of God they will either divinize man (i.e. make him – or some part thereof – into God[25]) or trivialize him (i.e. make him into less than what he is[26]).

Furthermore, we now see that Rist emphasizes equally the divine power/being, truth, and goodness/love not only because of human weakness (the surd-factor) and the way that the mind *just happens* to be structured, but because the latter structure participates in the ontological structure of the divine substance which stands to it as its Good. Therefore, we find in a more developed

---

22   For analysis of the structure, cogency, and aspects of the influence of Augustine's argument in *Trin.* 8-15 see B. David, "Anselm's Argument: the Augustinian Inheritance – Continuity and Development," *Augustinian Studies* 35: 1 (2004), 95–118.

23   For clarification see footnote # 7.

24   *N.b.* how a rigorous application of Platonic conceptions leads us to conclusions concurring with crucial aspects of Christian trinitarian doctrine. For arguments that are more exact see: Augustine's *Trin.* 8–15, Anselm's *Monologion*, and Bonaventure's *Itinerarium*.

25   Some might argue that Kant divinizes reason, Nietzsche divinizes the will, and Sartre divinizes man himself.

26   I think here of (*inter alia*) utilitarians, relativists, choice-theorists, and natural law theories that exclude God.

metaphysics an explicit balancing in the Godhead of being/power, truth, and love and, correspondingly, of the inclinations towards being/power, knowing, and loving in the mind. These are crucially important doctrines for as Rist shows us, incomplete accounts of God and/or of man will (i) fail to give us an acceptable explanation of human motivation and (ii) make the slide towards subordinationist theistic ethics – i.e. fideisms, rationalisms, and power-worship – and their secular imitations – found in Kantianism(s), utilitarianism, natural law theories without God, and choice-theory – both easier and more tempting.

However, if realist ethics is anchored in a God who is eternally self-causing/being, self-knowing, and self-loving *and* concretely united with "man," it will necessarily view man as one substance (i) in the image and likeness of God, (ii) made to be united with God, and (iii) governed by three primary inclinations ordered to the divine life. With lesser accounts of God (and man), we can certainly defeat Thrasymachus – Rist is right about that. But we stand in peril, at the same time, of (i) denying and/or defeating some crucial aspect of ourselves, and (ii) failing to possess the tools needed to diagnose our adversary's sickness and attempt a right and lasting cure. If man can only know and govern himself through knowing and loving God, there is simply no other way.

Finally, it seems fitting to measure our argument by a "Thomistically informed"[27] analysis of aspects of Aquinas" treatise on Law. This will allow us to understand better (i) that Thomas" doctrine of law – including his teaching on natural law – is a theistic ethic and (ii) perhaps also Rist's cryptic comment that Thomism is "that tradition in Western moral philosophy which presents the most detailed version of the realist theory of moral and spiritual life."[28]

Now, according to Thomas, each created substance exists by participation in a triune God governing all things by His eternal law, i.e. by Reason. Generally speaking, each living substance has (i) specific inclinations – participating in the divine inclinations – towards created goods (that participate in God), and (ii) a primary inclination – also ordered to God and in which the aforementioned inclinations participate. This inclination governs the secondary inclinations so that the creature, by following its desires for good, achieves its determinate end. Hence, the dog's desire for food, water, and play are ordered to its instinctive desire to actualize its potential as dog – according to which mode of existence it participates, without knowledge, in God. Unlike the irrational creature, however, man's inclinations to created goods are ordered – on account of his possession of reason (in which respect he stands in the image and likeness of God) – by an explicit inclination towards God Himself. This inclination is comprised of man's intellect and will/rational appetite. While intellect's proper end

---

27   By this I mean that I will read his account of law in the context of teachings presented elsewhere in the *Summa* on God, Man, and creation.
28   Rist, 281.

is God under the aspect of Truth, the will's proper end is God under the aspect of Good. Taken altogether, this means that man's (i) desires for such goods as food, procreation, community, and knowledge are ordered by his primary inclination to God, and (ii) determinate end consists in union with God. In other words, if man were not ordered to God he could not be ordered to created goods; and he is ordered to created goods so as to be ordered to God.[29] Thomas asserts, therefore, that insofar as man possesses reason, he is governed by *the law of reason*, viz. a natural law *implanted in him by God* ordering him to God. Man discovers this *divinely established law* by way of *synderesis*; its first precept is that "good is to be done and pursued and evil is to be avoided"; the secondary/explanatory precepts participate in the above and consist in pursuing what belongs to basic self-preservation, the preservation of the family, and (above all else) the good of reason – including society and God. Hence, God is *the alpha and the omega* of the natural law.

Thomas makes it clear, however, that governance by natural law constitutes only one aspect of man's participation in eternal law. This is because natural law, taken on its own, is an incomplete guide for human living. Although it will aid man thereto, it cannot bring him to his determinate end of union with God *since* reason and will are (i) limited in their scope – they cannot, on their own, know and will the divine essence – , and (ii) defective in their operations. Hence Thomas maintains, like Augustine, that human substance exists in a state of privation. As a "reformed"-Platonist, he understands that each person has some primordial/implicit awareness of God[30] and inclinations towards knowing the essence of God and achieving beatitude[31] but on account of our privative state we need, in addition to the natural law, God's direct help, viz. divine law, in order to achieve the knowledge, rectitude, and beatitude we innately desire. This law, implanted in us by grace/illumination, is inclusive of natural law and helps us to fulfill it. Moreover, divine law and human law (which is supposed to participate in natural law) have the overall function of enforcing, clarifying, and develop-

---

29   This shows why natural law doctrines that either exclude or are not anchored in God (the so-called "New Natural-Law Theory') are incomplete. For if man is not ordered to the Good itself there is no way to explain (amongst other things) the existence of "basic" goods, and man's need to order rightly his relation to them in the first place. *Contra* Finnis, it complicates the issue to list practical reasonableness as one of the seven basic goods since it is by this good, viz. reason – which is ordered to the Good itself! – that one orders one's relation to the other goods. (This would hold even if Finnis asserts that each basic good participates in God for in that case he will have denied the special/pre-eminent way that human reason participates in God.) There is no doubt, however, that his approach may be useful in certain contexts – as in helping people see their inclinations to good – and in clarifying aspects of natural law itself. *Cf.* Rist, 257–260.

30   *S.T.I.2.1, reply obj. 1.*

31   *S.T. I.12.1, respondeo;* and *II, 3,8, respondeo.*

ing natural law on the one hand, and teaching man what he needs to know and do to achieve beatitude on the other hand. For Thomas, then, *God's law for man* includes what he calls divine law, natural law, and human law; and taken altogether, these provide man with a sufficient guide for right living.

It is obvious, therefore, that Thomas" doctrine of law is essentially a theistic ethic having the same essential structure and philosophical presuppositions we sketched out earlier. The universe consists in an array of substances that participate, to greater and lesser degrees, in God; man stands in a state of privation with the result that the inclinations to God governing his rational element, viz. intellect and will, are less capable than they ought to be; despite their privations, intellect and will participate in some supreme "inclinations" in the Godhead; the rules for human right-living, viz. divine law, natural law, and human law, presuppose an eternal law that includes the ideal of union of human substance with divine substance; man receives the aforementioned laws – whether by indirect or direct illumination – by participation in God; and by his reason man is required to figure out and follow the implications of the law given to him by God. From beginning to end, Thomas's doctrine of law is grounded in philosophically satisfying accounts of God, participation, substance, mind, and evil as privation.

We conclude that Rist's argument for realist ethics is grounded in a coherent metaphysics, and that it can be strengthened by focusing not only on a more developed concept of God but also on the essential philosophical logic and related doctrines (like substance, participation, mind, and evil as privation) that sustain and develop it. This will provide us with accounts of God and of man that include and seek to integrate and unify the whole person with God. As a result, we will possess a satisfactory understanding of human motivation, and a way around the problem of de-humanization, viz. of focusing too much on one aspect of God and/or the human self to the exclusion of other equally important aspects, that characterizes (i) some forms of theistic ethics and (ii) each and every of their secular imitations.

Hence, as Plato shows us in the *Republic*, and as Rist eloquently reminds us in *Real Ethics*, Thrasymachus must be engaged and rebuffed not just by fine sounding concepts and clever counter-arguments but also by showing that the very ground of his judgment-making (epistemology) and the ontological structure of his mind and of reality as a whole are *realist*.[32] To follow Plato's example, we require not just a "reformed" account of the *Sun* (i.e. the likeness and offspring of the Good), but also "reformed" accounts of (i) the *Good Himself* and (ii) the *Line, Cave, and human person* that explain Him. We certainly need ethical doctrine that is grounded in *realist* metaphysics, but this metaphysics needs to be as cogent as possible and presented side by side with its concomitant psychology and epistemology.

---

32. Rist, 30.

The Choices of the Media Elite and the Moral Vision of Society

Armando Fumagalli

First of all, let me say that I agree with the principal theses explicated in Professor Rist's important and thoughtful book. I especially agree that the only coherent position in moral philosophy is realist and theistic.

Rist shows that it is impossible for us to have an ethics without metaphysics. This important point should not pass unnoticed. Rist stresses the importance of giving a foundation to rules and of examining the reason why we consider rationality a condition of goodness. He argues that it is not sufficient to refer to an act's conformity with rationality in order to qualify it as a good act. A philosopher should also ground the relation between rationality and human nature, and answer the question why rationality should be an end in itself.

I would like especially to emphasize the place of love in this moral proposal. Without any "romantic" magniloquence, but in crucial points of the book and quite often, Professor Rist says that love is essential to man's morality. He comes to this conclusion not only through the Thomistic view, according to which virtues are modes of love. He also shows that in many fields of life strict justice does not suffice because it does not reach the particular personal level to which every human being legitimately desires to be considered (see, *e.g.*, p. 130). Love is the unifying force that counters the tendencies to division and self-destruction that affect human life.

In what follows, I will use my specific professional expertise to comment on some other points of the book that I much appreciated and that are closer to my field, which is semiotics and the narrative of cinema and television.

In particular, I want to focus both on how society accepts moral reasons and on how to communicate moral arguments to non-specialists who make up the vast majority in a society.

As is well known, in the last few decades some of the leading philosophers in moral theory have reconsidered the importance of narrative in the moral education of a community. Alasdair MacIntyre remains a major figure. I would include also Charles Taylor, as well as Martha Nussbaum – although I do not agree with some of what she regards as important consequences of her view. In Italy, we have had some very important books by Giuseppe Abbà.[1] As far as the French language is concerned, I should mention the theological research of Servais Pinckaers,[2] and, among German philosophers, the beautiful works of Robert Spaemann.[3]

Real Ethics, although it does not make it the object of specific thematic reflections, shows an important and vivid awareness of the problem of the distinction between, on the one hand, an intellectual and media elite of society – which has access to pure reflection, teaches in universities, writes in journals, magazines and newspapers and inspires cinema and television – and, on the other hand, all the other parts of society (the great majority) which are *de facto* inspired and guided by this elite. In developed societies, the majority of people is greatly under-represented in media. The intellectual elite has a strong gatekeeping role. The media is almost everywhere the expression of a culturally radical minority that owns the access to the articulation of the contents and tends to represent and express itself much more strongly than the other social groups.

Among the most impressive pages of *Real Ethics*, are perhaps those dedicated to the crisis of democracy and its ethical insufficiency as reduced only to a system of voting. This system is not supported by a high degree of information, participation, and concern at every level of social and public life: "So long as we have free choice, we believe that we can achieve our status as human beings; so long as we live in a 'democratic' society, we believe we have the structure within which we can be 'free.' If choice is the idolatry of private life, democracy has become the idolatry of public life" (248). The following passage gives a severe, but I think not exaggerated, description of the risk faced by modern society: "For it is to be noted that some of the goals of Hitler, Stalin and other promoters of man remade can be achieved in a more anodyne but equally mindless society, the more comfortable totalitarianism of egalitarian, because rootless and envious individualism. It is no accident that such individualism, coupled with ignorance and contempt for the past, can flourish under some versions of the 'democratic' umbrella; indeed such characteristics may become the

---

1 See Giuseppe Abbà, *Felicità, vita buona e virtù: Saggio di filosofia morale* (Roma: Las, 1989); *Quale impostazione per la filosofia morale?* (Roma: LAS, 1996). Abbà is very attentive to the American debate in ethics.

2 See especially Servais Th. Pinckaers, O.P., *The Sources of Christian Morality (1985)*, trans. Sr. Mary Thomas Noble, O.P. (Washington, D.C.: Catholic University of America Press, 1995); *La morale catholique* (Paris: Les Éditions du Cerf/Fides, 1991).

3 See Robert Spaemann, *Basic Moral Concepts* (1986), trans. T. J. Armstrong (London and New York: Routledge, 1989); *Glück und Wohlwollen* (Stuttgart: Ernst Klett, 1989).

illusory Three Pillars of any future 'democracy' itself: driven by class divisions, devastated by crime, corrupt in its political dealings and judicial processes, massively philistine and illiterate (though led by a highly articulate, educated and sophisticated elite), tasteless and brutal in its entertainment – and self-devoted to 'freedom' viewed as choice. The United States has moved far in this direction and Canadians, being next in line and now comparatively unprotected, have much to fear beyond their present anxieties about separatism" (249).

I think that this big and impressive division between the intellectual elite, on the one hand, and the vast majority of people, on the other – a division not always fully considered by intellectuals, who normally live with, and are friends and relatives of, other intellectuals – has some interesting consequences that should be considered:

1. Some moral problems that we tend to consider universal actually represent only 2–3% of the population that constitutes this elite.

2. At the same time, this elite is responsible for the construction of the imaginary landscape – *l'imaginaire*, as French philosophers and sociologists called it in the Sixties – that affects 95% of the population. It affects it with various degrees of deepness and effectiveness, depending on how much the stories, values, and characters differ from the traditional *credo* of a community, on how long this kind of construction has been represented, etc. For example, the large acceptance of homosexuality in most European and north-American societies is the result of more or less ten years of strong propaganda in favor of the homosexual lifestyle. This lifestyle – after some years of preparation in art film and in selected intellectual circles – has reached first the mainstream cinema and second the television – beginning in 1993 with the film *Philadelphia*, a masterpiece of ideological rhetoric and propaganda, and then with *In and Out* and many other movies that pushed forward this agenda.

3. As I just mentioned, the moral attitudes of the intellectual elites reach most of the population when they are mediated by, but I should better say embodied in, stories with passion, emotions, and *big* characters: namely, stories endowed with that profound dimension which turns them into powerful and effective metaphors of life.[4] This field is open to good and to evil, right and wrong. Although I am convinced, as Aristotle expressed in the *Rhetoric*,[5] that truth has a force in itself, and that a true argument is, by its nature, stronger than a false one, I have to say that, unfortunately, in the last decades false arguments have found many very

---

4   For the story as a metaphor of life see the thoughtful reflection by Robert McKee, *Story: Substance, Structure, Style, and the Principles of Screenwriting* (New York: HarperCollins, 1997). McKee expresses, in a more clear, profound, and effective way, something that we could find also in Paul Ricoeur and in some very interesting works by C. S. Lewis, such as some essays collected in C. S. Lewis, *On This and Other Worlds* (London: Fount, 2000).

5   Aristotle, *Rhetoric*, 1355a.

skilful rhetoricians – especially in cinema, TV fiction and the media – while true ones seem to have more difficulty finding good spokespersons.

4. I am convinced that today most people in the world – including North American and European countries – still have a strong sense of the natural values of life (those expressed in the Ten Commandments), and that an intense anti-education made by the media can have an important influence, but cannot completely sweep away the basics of this moral sense. In Italy, we had in the Seventies a very intense pro-abortion campaign in the press, which simply declared it to be woman's right; but now that the campaign is no longer as active and as intense as it was during those years, the natural truth of abortion as a trauma for the woman and the destruction of a new life is coming out into the open.

From a different angle, it is interesting to note that in the top spots of the world cinema box office – that is, the movies that have gained more at the box office – there are movies showing a view of life in substantial – and sometimes in strong and explicit – accordance with a theistic and realist ethics.[6] I like to mention not only *Titanic*, which would deserve specific explanations and distinctions, but also *The Lord of the Rings* (an adaptation of a great Christian novel), *Harry Potter*, *Spider Man*, *Forrest Gump*, etc. Regrettably, this tradition and its acceptance are little by little menaced by the elite's products.

Remaining in the field of cinema, we might recall movies like *American Beauty* and the recent Oscar-winning *The Hours* (which contains a sort of elegy to suicide), which have not been big hits at the American box office, but which are big hits in some secularised and more intellectualised European countries. We could also think of some TV shows that are targeted mainly to audiences of young cultured professionals; an example is *Friends*, which, with its nihilist approach, reaches specific audiences of young bright people all over the world.[7]

Regarding this division between the large traditional audience and what is currently proposed to young intellectuals, it can be useful to consider that in Italy, over the last few years, the top TV shows dealt with stories adapted from the Bible and with biographies of saints – like Padre Pio (a Franciscan recently canonized by the Pope) or the blessed Pope John XXIII. These were excellent products, very well written, which, in a country with six main channels competing every night for the audience, managed to reach the impressive viewer share of more than 40%, and in the case of the *biopic* of Pope John XXIII more than 50%. These TV shows have shown in an extremely clear – I would say, in a shocking – way that if you are able to tell well a story about God, prayer, sin and forgiveness, confession and holy Mass, etc., people will be eager to hear it. I will come back to this question soon. But, now, let's go back to Rist's book.

---

6   The first who showed this truth has been Michael Medved in his very influential book, *Hollywood vs. America* (New York: Harper Collins, 1993).

7   For a brilliant analysis of the anthropological content of some popular American TV series, see Paolo Braga, *Dal Personaggio allo Spettatore* (Milano: Angeli, 2003).

One of the main challenges of contemporary philosophy to realist and theistic morals is the position that makes choice an absolute. In the real lives of our contemporaries it is a minority position; but it is gaining force and effectiveness through a corruption that has a great appeal today: namely, the absolutization of the figure of the artist as the new exceptional individual, as the new saint, as the man who has such a special sensitiveness that allows him to *see* indefectibly what is worth doing and living. In *Real Ethics*, this view is shortly but perfectly described (190). I cannot dwell on the characteristics and the roots of this mentality, but I would like to recall Charles Taylor's reflections in *Sources of the Self* (and in a much shorter book that has been published under two different titles: *The Malaise of Modernity* and *The Ethics of Authenticity*).[8] Taylor shows very well how deep are the roots of this mentality, and he gives reasons to think that it is going to be more and more diffused. Let me also refer to an English scholar, Colin Campbell, who in a very suggestive study[9] stresses with subtlety that this way of thinking grows from an exasperated imagination. This imagination nurtures bohemian ideals, and inspires individuals who dream to be artists (and may live this ideal in the evening and on weekends) while being, at the same time, totally integrated in a bourgeois and technocratic system of organization of work. How could we not see here the elite lives of most of the "yuppies" in many European countries and – as far as I know – of urban and suburban Americans?

John Rist has some important arguments against the glorification of choice as an end in itself (200 ff). I think that these arguments touch upon a main problem of our societies, especially as far as the elites are concerned. The absolutization of choice can lead to such extremes as suicide and homicide. It is crucial to make people aware of this – as Rist does in his book (221). One of the reasons why I mentioned the movie *The Hours* is that its vision of suicide represents a very revealing example of the direction towards which a certain "artistic" mentality is going.

But, as we must make a conclusion, let us consider very shortly four possible consequences of what we have been saying.

a. First of all, if we want a moral view to reach society in a shorter amount of time than the centuries normally needed for the moral philosopher's elaborations to reach a relevant part of civilization, it is extremely important that we get more familiar with studying and elaborating stories. Most of the greatest moral systems (including the Christian ones) have come to us through stories – real

8   Charles Taylor, *Sources of the Self: The Making of Modern Identity* (Cambridge, Mass.: Harvard University Press, 1989); *The Malaise of Modernity* or *The Ethics of Authenticity* (Cambridge, Mass.: Harvard University Press, 1991).
9   Colin Campbell, *The Romantic Ethic and the Spirit of Modern Consumerism* (Oxford: Blackwell, 1987).

stories like that of Jesus, the Prophets and the Apostles, and allegories and parables like those that the Lord told us in the Gospel. It was only at a second moment that people reflected on them and shaped both a set of dogmas and the theoretical synthesis of the various catechisms. For those who are Christian, it is very important never to forget that the abstract and systematic way of understanding and transmitting wisdom and attitudes always has *de facto* a minority – a very important, but minority – dimension, only attainable by a certainly crucial but numerically very slight elite. The incredible (before it appeared: *ab esse ad posse valet illatio*) amplitude and velocity of the spreading of a narrative phenomenon like *Harry Potter* should help us to see how fast a narrative, with its characters and its values, can today reach people all over the world. This phenomenon can also help us to consider how important it is that Christian intellectuals, Christian universities, and men who think it their duty to promote a vision of life according to Christian values feel responsible to promote also in the field of narratives (i.e., literature, comics, cinema, TV fiction, etc.) a free but profound elaboration of passionate and modern stories embodying a transcendent vision of life: stories showing – as in the great literature of Dostoevsky and Shakespeare – the greatness and weakness of man, his being a creature of God, his desire for the good, and the destruction that evil brings to human lives.

b. Second, it would be of great interest to moral philosophers to confront themselves more with the theoretical and practical reflection involved in constructing stories: especially with the treasure of professional skills and practical wisdom that we can find in people who work for mainstream cinema. The interviews with great screenwriters, which appear in professional magazines like *Creative Screenwriting*, and the books collecting experiences of those professionals, contain usually remarkable anthropological and moral insights.[10] We might think of the stories written for big audiences as some sort of condensed moral experiences. And if we have the skill to analyse the audience's reaction in terms of acceptance (even to the point of enthusiasm) or rejection of those experiences, we can use the stories to make moral experiments, as if they were case studies for applied ethics. We certainly should try to understand the force of a story by isolating it from other elements, such as directing, acting, music, etc. But, it is essential to finally focus on the deep reasons for the enormous success and profound impact of movies like *Forrest Gump, Braveheart, A Beautiful*

---

10   See, for example, Joel Engel (ed.), *Screenwriters on Screenwriting* (New York: Hyperion, 1995); Joel Engel (ed.), *Oscar-Winning Screenwriters on Screenwriting* (New York: Hyperion, 2002); William Goldman, *Adventures in the Screentrade* (New York: Warner Books, 1983); William Goldman, *Which Lie did I Tell? More Adventures in the Screen Trade* (London: Bloomsbury, 2000). As is well known, most great screenwriters are Jews; for reason that I do not know – maybe the biblical tradition of great narrative – they seem to have a special gift in telling stories both entertaining and profound.

Mind, Monsters, Inc., Gladiator and *Erin Brockovich*. At the heart of every story there is a moral dilemma; and normally it is not an easy dilemma between a clear good and an evident evil, but a subtle dilemma between two non-compatible goods or between two forms of evil. The spine of the stories narrated in the great popular movies of our time are moral dilemmas: i.e., problems of characters who have to answer to difficult situations. This is what we love and appreciate about them. And it is a common truth on which there is full agreement among people who write for the cinema as well as among those who teach how to do it.[11]

c. My third point relates to what Rist says on pages 246–247 of his book, when he reflects on the always provisional and fragile unity of societies like the United States and Canada, with their different modes of integration. Unity and cooperation in a specific society are always the result of an education that goes deep into the feelings of people, helping them to understand – and to *feel* – why they are a country, what *foundational* values they share, etc. A strong confrontation with some errors and extremisms of a part of the Islamic tradition should help us see that every state of a complex and peaceful society is possible because people share a vision of human nature: a vision of life. The result is a strong confirmation of the importance of education, through the *great stories*, as we have been saying, but also through every institution and medium that modern societies have found convenient to transmit the values of a culture. Before teaching skills for specific jobs or professions, we ought to transmit the values that are at the foundation of our community and of our society.

d. The fourth and last point is about the importance of some specific aspects of the modern sensibility. Young generations are growing up with a very intense training in stories. They watch thousands of stories on television and in the theatres. And one of the effects of this intensive training is the capacity to increase the response of empathy for people's problems. The new generations are more sensitive to the problems of other people, and in general of every person, but they normally have no clues about how to give real answers and solutions to the dilemmas of life. They have sympathy but do not have the capacity to show how to reach a good human life.

In this context, I think that the personalist (but metaphysically founded) turn made by Pope John Paul II in moral philosophy and moral theology is very

---

11   This is a point on which there is a complete agreement among the professionals who teach screenwriting and work as consultants for many important companies. Let me recall here at least the names of Robert McKee, Linda Seger, John Truby, and Chris Vogler. In literature, it is a statement held with special clarity by Wayne Booth, *The Rhetoric of Fiction*, 2nd edition (Chicago: University of Chicago Press, 1983). See also Wayne Booth, *The Company We Keep: An Ethics of Fiction* (Berkeley, Los Angeles, London: University of California Press, 1988), and Gianfranco Bettetini and Armando Fumagalli, *Quel che resta dei media*

important. From his book of 1960, *Love and Responsibility*, on, he tried to understand moral problems in the context of a realist – in Rist's sense – ethics: that is, from the point of view of the moral agent. This shift in the point of view – which is not related by chance to the long and deep affection and intellectual training of the young Karol Wojtyla in literature and in drama: a passion which made him decide to be a professional literary man and a man of the theatre – is greatly sympathetic with contemporary mentality because it helps to show clearly and effectively how moral solutions are the real *solutions* to the drama of life. Moral solutions are not the superimposed laws of a detached and lonely Sovereign, but – as John Rist suggests in his beautiful book – proposals made by a loving God Who wants our good.

I think that a profound acquaintance with John Paul II's theological reflection can help Christians see ways to make our moral view more friendly and acceptable to our contemporaries. This acquaintance can also help us understand another of the points stated by Rist: namely, the insufficiency of justice and the necessity of love. Bishop Wojtyla was one of the main inspirers of key pages of a crucial document of the Second Vatican Council. I am thinking of the part of the document *Gaudium et spes* in which we find a synthesis of Christian anthropology. More specifically, n. 24 reads, "man, who is the only creature on earth which God willed for itself (*sola creatura est quam Deus propter seipsam voluerit*), cannot fully find himself except through a sincere gift of himself (*plene seipsum invenire non posse nisi per sincerum sui ipsius donum*)." I think that there is still room to work out the consequences of this anthropological thesis of the Second Vatican Council, which helps us to go in depth into, and hopefully to develop, John Rist's call for an ethics where knowledge of reality as a gift from the loving God opens to the intelligent love that is the essence of all moral action.

A Response to Commentators

John M. Rist

Before offering a response to the revised comments of Professors Dauphinais, David, Fumagalli, and McInerny, I may perhaps be allowed to reflect – briefly and not entirely irrelevantly – on the fate of *Real Ethics* since its publication. All four of my present commentators have been both kind and constructive, as have the great majority of the reviewers; perhaps more informative is that the openly hostile reception I thought the book might meet in other quarters has not materialized. My hard-core opponents and the journals they control have for the most part not bothered to review it: a far more effective way of encouraging themselves and others to avoid the challenge I hoped the book would offer – and an indication of the gulf between secular and non-secular, transcendental and non-transcendental modern thought to which I drew attention.

But now to my present response: Dauphinais and McInerny are primarily concerned to draw attention to what they take to be my comparative injustice to or inaccuracy about Aristotle and Aquinas respectively; David has argued that my case would be stronger if I had offered a more detailed account of the God I urged is necessary for serious moral theorizing, while Fumagalli has concerned himself with some practical aspects of the gulf I outlined between the views of our modern Western élites and the vast mass of the public whom they have gradually desensitized into an acceptance of less and less "traditional" lifestyles through a media saturated with images of homosexuality, suicide, murder and other "bohemian" forms of behavior – all signed and sealed with the stamp of the Goddess Choice and her perversely "democratic" reflections in the public domain.

All of my present commentators are sympathetic; none belongs to that group I was primarily challenging when I wrote *Real Ethics*: the professionals who are unwilling to face the consequences of the fundamental weaknesses of any non-theistic position in ethics. And I say "position" in the singular because I wanted to argue, crudely, that there is a significant sense in which all non-theistic positions in ethics are ultimately identical: that is, that they want to found a morality-substitute on the more or less rational choices and decisions of human beings, often with blithe disregard of our weaknesses both intellectual and moral. And having urged that central point I wanted to add that we do not make the situation better if, in default of a theistic foundation we state that there is no need for foundations anyway (like Rawls) or that our situation is now so difficult that in the absence of foundations we should follow Sidgwick or more recently McDowell and Blackburn in *pretending* that certain "quasi-realist" foundations exist when in fact they do not – in other words, that the best route to a good set of moral behaviors is to start with deception on matters allowed to be of the greatest importance. I rather regret that my present commentators only make brief allusion to the contemporary "moral" need to lie and deceive.

Those basic points made, however, let me turn to the present comments; first those of Michael Dauphinais. Dauphinais' basic objection is to my treatment of Aristotle, and let me start by trying to clear away a possible source of confusion. As a moral philosopher, I placed Aristotle between Platonic metaphysical morality and the theories of contemporary practical reasoners. I did not suggest, however, that Aristotle would wish to reduce ethics to practical reasoning or that his "third-person" stance and metaphysical concerns with the unity of the human agent rather than with our uniquely moral character indicate any acceptance on his part of a morally neutral universe. My point was (and is) that Aristotle's non-moral God and his apparent neglect of providence (Early Christians on this latter ground often considered him an atheist), coupled with his abandonment of Platonic Forms, leave him reliant on shadows of Platonism (such as the notion that the moral agent does things "for the sake of 'the fine'" [*to kalon*]), which, being apparently free-floating, might seem easily dispensable to those wishing to push his ontological account of human nature to a more extreme and value-free resolution. So the problem is less that Aristotle does not ground his ethics on metaphysics (despite his own reasonable concerns with the autonomy of ethical analysis), than with the inability of his "ontology" to account for moral agency rather than, say, prudential judgment.

As Aristotle himself says in the *Politics* (1253a), reason enables man to identify what is beneficial and what is not, hence what is just and what is unjust. But what has now become of the foundations of specifically moral obligation? (And I always wonder why Aristotle so consistently ignores almost everything Plato says about love and inspiration.) Certainly the Aristotelian good is what all men desire (or think they desire), but are such desires in themselves sufficient guarantee for the performance of moral acts (or for acts to be moral)? As we shall see, similar difficulties arise over Aquinas's *inclinationes*.

Hence to Dauphinais' question as to whether "the overall project of Aristotle works in a similar manner [to that of Plato] in justifying a moral realism," my reply is that Aristotle thinks it does, but he has not shown that it does; indeed that he cannot show that it does because he has loosened some of the Platonic timbers necessary to make the moral house stand. Aristotle himself is certainly not a contemporary practical reasoner, but – both by default and by his philosophical virtue in improving on Plato's account of our ontological unity – he has given succor to those who are, as subsequent and contemporary history has borne out.

Dauphinais thinks that my remark in *Real Ethics* that Aristotle has concentrated on man as a metaphysical unity rather than as a divided moral subject is a "weak criticism," since if Aristotle's account of *akrasia* will not do, the same can be said of the lack of metaphysical unity – the failure to solve the soul-body problem – in Plato. I would agree with that comment on Plato – and indeed to a considerable extent it could also be applied to Augustine, though Augustine seems to have realized the difficulty without being able to solve it. But my point is that though Plato is limited in his anthropology – verging towards the position that the pure soul is simply us – the threat to morals from an ultra-Aristotelianism is even greater, for two reasons: first, that Aristotle does not directly deal with the possibility that we might live in a value-free universe; second, that his account of God can readily be held to entail (or allow for) an immanentist version of naturalism in ethics. Like Kant's "things in themselves," Aristotle's God can be easily scrapped.

Dauphinais links his complaints about my treatment of Aristotle with more wide-ranging suggestions that I propose "an apparent rejection of the intellectual component of the moral life" and that the "anti-intellectual thrust of [my] argument contains significant risks." In my reaction against intellectualist accounts of human nature I have put too much emphasis on the "moral self." My reply is that if that is indeed what I did in *Real Ethics*, it is certainly not what I intended. I do not regard my position as anti-intellectual any more than it is anti-voluntarist: my Augustinian claim is that both the mind and the emotions are subject to their post-lapsarian weaknesses: *ignorantia* and *concupiscentia*. And I would add that if I am anti-intellectual in opposing a post-Cartesian account of passionless reason, I am pro-intellectual in advocating a Platonically "erotic" mind: a mind, that is, which in us cannot be separated from its perverse or wholesome desires.

Let me now turn to McInerny, whose comments are broadly concerned with the possibility of moral conversion and progress, and more specifically whether in misrepresenting Aquinas's account of the end of the human person, I have made it difficult to see how such progression is intelligible in the "natural" order. McInerny argues that my conclusions on such matters are "unimpeachable from the standpoint of supernatural truth, but leave the unbeliever, or even the Christian concerned with philosophical arguments, wondering what place there is in this narrative of liberation for the *natural* knowledge of the human good." In so arguing McInerny makes a specific kind of distinction between man's natural and supernatural ends, and maintains that although our natural end is ordered to our supernatural end, a proper understanding of a natural end enables us to identify "some basic and shared truths that not even a lifelong prisoner to modern moral philosophy could dispute." This is in a sense another version of an attack on my supposed "anti-intellectualism," in that in my version of the ordering of our natural to our supernatural end we may seem to be unable to make moral progress without the specifically theological virtues.

Let me make another distinction. I certainly did not want to say that those without any understanding of the theological virtues cannot make moral progress. What I do claim is that an adequate *justification* of the moral order is impossible without reference to such virtues (and therefore to God) and that those who make progress in an explicitly atheist world do so only with the help of a divine grace which is in fact urging them not merely towards our apparently natural end but to our actual and ultimate supernatural end.

What worries McInerny is that, in talking about growth towards a "soul," I seem to claim that in our fallen state we have no common starting point whereby – in virtue of what Aquinas calls our *inclinationes* – we always have a basic grasp of the good to which we should aspire. But if I suggested that, I would accept McInerny's criticism: I certainly do not advocate the Calvinist view that we are totally depraved; indeed I suspect that if we were totally depraved we could not exist. What I did say, however, as McInerny recognizes, is that our *inclinationes* are seriously damaged by both *ignorantia* and *concupiscentia*, and I think I would add that this has probably been the case (as Augustine saw) ever since we were conceived or had any sort of awareness of the moral space we inhabit, and that in advancing from our second-nature dividedness we are advancing (however it may seem) not only to a hypothetical "natural" end but to the supernatural end to which we are in fact called. It is difficult to avoid being theological at this point, but it seems that our hypothetical natural end cannot be secure; some version of it was not even secure in the case of Adam and Eve. They reached a condition of being able not to sin, a state inferior to that of being unable to sin. Benedict Ashley, to whom I was much indebted in this section of *Real Ethics*, says that "the human person even in our existential order has a natural finality which is ultimate in its own order." I would say that in our existential order we might have had such a natural finality and if, *per impossibile*, God were to change his mind about the mode of our nature and salvation, we might have it again, but as it stands it is only an unrealizable possibility.

So I agree with McInerny that we have a real though difficult chance of moral growth because we have some sickened version of a real "soul" from the time of our conception. Where I hesitate about what I take to be the view of McInerny – and probably also of Aquinas – is over the present state of our *inclinationes*. The argument here is empirical; it concerns the degree of damage done to our *inclinationes* by the society in which we are conceived and live our lives, for many of our *inclinationes* are to the apparent, not the real good. Hence our

difficulty, theoretical as well as practical, is to determine where the real good
lies. It is true, as perhaps McInerny implies, that we all seem to have a pre-philosophical sense of the good, even of the transcendent good; indeed this "sense"
is what philosophers like Mackie think needs to be dissipated by some kind of
error theory – precisely because it is pre-philosophical. In reply to Mackie, however, we must account not only for our pre-philosophical intimations of the
Good, but also (equally importantly) for the fact that it is so easily subverted.
Such an account would probably have to place greater weight than Aquinas
allowed on the fact that most of our contemporary *inclinationes* are the product
of the multifarious varieties of evil with which our choice-driven society is able
to supply us. And among such offerings not the least is the regular denial by our
élites of the notion of truth itself. For many modern philosophers the only truth
is that there is no truth; McInerny, however, rightly but counter-culturally, refers
to "naturally known truths."

Let me now move from those who want to reformulate parts of what I have
said to those more concerned to progress further down the road I have traveled.
Barry David holds that to make my case stronger I need a more fully developed,
indeed more specifically Christian and Trinitarian account of God. I am sure
that is true, and I offered only the basics in *Real Ethics*, largely because my primary aim was to do a Socratic demolition job on theories which substitute the
primacy of choice (rational or not) for the primacy of goodness. I thus allowed
myself only a limited sketch of the metaphysical preconditions of a defense of
realist ethics as such, hoping also that without in any way concealing my
Christianity I might to appeal a little more readily to those readers who find
specifically Christian themes particularly offensive. But if much of my demolition work could be accepted I would be happy to proceed on many of the lines
advocated by David.

There is perhaps a problem about how full an account of God would be the
most effective. David thinks that a useful version would stress in the first
instance God's perfections as power, being/goodness and truth. Again I have no
quarrel with that – except that I would wish to be careful not to put to much
emphasis on divine power, since a mere cringing before God is hardly the mark
of a loving creature, even though some rather eminent philosophers, not least
Peter Geach, talk at times as if that is the best we can hope for. But as I said more
than once in *Real Ethics*, to offer a portrait of a tyrannical God is the best way
of generating theories of religiously-based tyranny among God's agents.
Muslims and Calvinists, beware.

David also raises the question of other divine perfections, of which perhaps
the most interesting is beauty. It is a matter of historical fact that it took some
time for the early Christians to recognize beauty as a divine attribute, and we
must credit direct Platonic influence for much of that recognition – along with

the Platonically interpreted *Song of Songs* by Origen and his successors. It is interesting, though beyond the scope of my present response, to notice how a Platonizing emphasis on beauty helped ancient Christians (and many but not all of their later successors) to avoid the appellation "enemies of the good and the beautiful" which pagan Platonists were inclined to bestow on them – not least because they were so concerned about the dangers of sensuality as to be blinded to the true beauty of God and man his image, preferring a more puritanical, even at times near-Talibanish, hostility to any beauty which might seem too "bodily": a theme to which in the future I hope to return.

In an earlier draft of his response David commented in a somewhat Procline fashion on non-participated eternal distinctions in God. My own reading of this, if I were to develop it further, would be that virtue-terms have a focal reference, that is, that they are *pros hen* equivocals, but that it is a necessary part of a realist metaphysics to say that in introducing focal reference we are talking not only about focal *meaning* but also about *derivation* from a primary principle. And it would be helpful in considering focal meaning to look again at the hopefully intelligible doctrine of man as created in the image and likeness of God: a doctrine which, rather shamefully, has hardly been developed intellectually since Patristic times, though development is merely assumed in contemporary theological documents. Here I raise, without answering, the matter of what should be the modern response to the old Patristic view that it is problematic whether or not women are created in the image and likeness of God.

I turn finally to Fumagalli, whose comments are of a rather different order: sociological rather than metaphysical, but no less constructive for that. Although Fumagalli concludes – there is some similarity here to David's approach – with advice to follow John Paul II's personalism in the attempt to make a realist ethic more palatable to our contemporaries, the larger part of his comment is dedicated to the distinction I drew between the concerns of the élite few and the more passive and often ignorant role of the silent majority who, he thinks, are able to feel sympathy when reading or seeing narratives but remain unfitted to propose real answers and solutions to the dilemmas of life such narratives reveal.

Perhaps, however, Fumagalli is too sanguine about particular features of the modern moral world which inhibit any significant movement from sympathy to sense. Let me comment on just a few of his specific observations in the hope that the general lines of a fuller response may become visible:

1. I accept that in Italy lots of people watch documentaries such as that on Pope John XXIII. But the example is illuminating. When talking to people who watched that film I frequently got the reaction, "Ah, yes, 'il papa buono,' he was not at all typical; that is not the oppressive institutional church that we know." In other words, John XXIII can be sophistically dismissed as virtually "anti-Catholic."

2. Fumagalli mentioned our "confrontation with some errors and extrem-

isms of a part of the Islamic tradition." I do not want to labor the point, but in such matters there is a strong tendency to give opponents the benefit of too many important doubts: there is an unwillingness both among Western élites and among frightened or demoralized Western Christians to face the fact that the problem with Islam is not simply with minor errors and extremism. It lies with the nature of the religion itself. Shari'a law, in its various manifestations, is incompatible with Christian ethics, not to say secular Western ethics. If we wish to compare Christianity with Islam we would do better to compare modern Islam with the Christianity of those who preached the Crusades than with the peace-loving, often exaggeratedly pacifist Christians of the 21st century. Facts are important here and it is worth asking why Christianity and philosophy (with much help from Aquinas) found a *modus vivendi*, while philosophy and Islam did not. In admitting, as I do, the achievement of Arabic philosophy up to the 12th century, I also ask why it is that after the 12th century there is little more than Western transplants.

3. I was interested in what Fumagalli said about homosexuality, and noted his proper comment that for the last ten years or so we have been subjected to strong propaganda in favor of the homosexual lifestyle. I want to use this point to attack another commonplace, and in my view, fallacious, assumption of much Western thought: that is the supposed ability radically to distinguish between the public and the private, so that it is claimed that what one does with one's homosexual partner in the bedroom or bath-house has no connection with the kind of social policies a homosexual politician may want to promote in the Cabinet Office. And the encouragement of a homosexual ethic is not merely giving free choice in the bedroom, it is familiarizing more and more people with the false notion that all partnerships are equally worthy.

In *Real Ethics* (144) I cited some remarks of a British journalist to the effect that current discussions of surrogacy "illustrate with chilling clarity how far this society has traveled towards a universal suspension of repugnance and an apparently limitless capacity to tolerate the intolerable." In the analogous matter of homosexuality there is good reason to believe that the more any supposed equality of worth between heterosexual and homosexual unions is purveyed, the less respect there will be for marriage and the traditional family – which is not a merely private matter but something affecting the moral, spiritual, social and economic life of us all. And of course, in terms of "Real Ethics," the exaggerated cult of privacy (tied to the radical distinction between public and private life) can only increase the divisions in the soul (not to speak of the lies in the soul) which as a member of the honorable company of Platonists I tried to deplore in *Real Ethics*.

ON RUSSELL HITTINGER'S
THE FIRST GRACE

Grace or Nature First?

Robert A. Gahl, Jr.

At the end of his introductory essay in *The First Grace: Rediscovering the Natural Law in a Post-Christian World*, Russell Hittinger proposes criteria required to advance natural law theory in today's post-Christian culture. The proposed criteria challenge common presuppositions for scholarly discussion today about natural law. To understand the problem of natural law, Hittinger proposes that we must get beyond arguments pointing to or issuing from moral premises and address the underlying, foundational questions that are presupposed by such moral arguments. What is unusual and provocative about Hittinger's proposal is the foundational and speculative depth to which he invites his reader. Hittinger contends that the future of natural law theory depends upon nothing less than "considerations of anthropology and theology" (xlvi).

The first chapter, entitled *Natural Law and Catholic Moral Theology*, begins his theological discussion of natural law with the express intent of clarifying current disagreement among Catholic moralists and stimulating ecumenical dialogue by convincing Protestants that the Catholic natural law tradition was developed within a context of deeply textured theological considerations. To begin his analysis of the theological presuppositions of traditional conceptions of natural law, Hittinger describes the three dimensions or, as he calls them, foci, of natural law: (1) law in the human mind, (2) law in nature, and (3) law in the mind of God. With the enumeration of these three foci, Hittinger displays the epistemic, anthropic, and theonomic aspects embraced by the traditional understanding of natural law. He then proceeds with an extraordinarily strong emphasis on the importance of the third, that is the theonomic, throughout the tradition of natural law theories.

In this commentary on *The First Grace*, I will take advantage of the extraordinary opportunity of this public debate to challenge Hittinger to clarify and illustrate some of the implications of his reading of Thomas Aquinas for the future of natural law theories in general and in particular for promoting ecumenical dialogue between Catholics and Protestants. To clarify my own position, I remain deeply sympathetic to the theological concerns brought to the fore by Hittinger and I agree with the bulk of his claims. But *The First Grace* provokes us to go further and to ask even deeper questions about the naturalness and the legality of natural law.

I will contend that *The First Grace* raises, without resolving, questions regarding the requirements for the promulgation of natural law. More specifically, *The First Grace* does not fully resolve the question of what one must know in order to be a subject of the natural law in a way proper to rational human nature. Another unresolved issue within *The First Grace* regards the differential characterization of the natural knowledge of God required for a human to be fully under the natural law and the theological requirements for being also subject to the New Law. Or, to put it more simply, *The First Grace* leaves unresolved the determination of the difference between what a human must know in order to fulfill the natural law and what he or she must do in order to receive sanctifying grace. With this critical commentary, I hope to help induce the author to clarify some of his claims regarding the anthropology and the theology presupposed by natural law theory and to further expound upon their implications. If I succeed, my success may be some small show of gratitude for all that I have learned from his work.

In *The First Grace,* Hittinger makes two controversial contentions regarding the divine character of natural law. First, he holds that only recently have the epistemic and anthropic dimensions of natural law been regarded as architectonic foci.[1] And second, he affirms that: "As a law, natural law is not 'in' nature or the human mind, but is rather in the mind of God" (11).

Much of *The First Grace* is a sustained argument in favor of divine command as a requirement for the legal character of natural law. In contrast with many of today's most prolific promoters of natural law theory but in perfect fidelity to the Thomistic texts, Hittinger forcefully argues that if natural law's legal exigencies were not first in God's mind, then the natural law would be no law at all. While carefully avoiding any implications of divine voluntarism, Hittinger reminds us that the natural law may be best defined according to its position within the descending order of being. When we consider things according to that which is first in reality, or according to ontological causes, natural law is, certainly, first and foremost from God.

Since it participates in the eternal law, natural law is, somehow, first in God's mind. I say *somehow* first in God's mind because while natural law as law must be from God, I wonder to what extent a faithful interpreter of Thomas can assert, as it seems to me that Hittinger does, that the natural law, *qua* natural law,

---

1   *See The First Grace*, 5: "Until recently, the proposition that natural law is chiefly a theological issue was uncontroversial in Catholic moral theology. Natural law in the human mind and natural law in nature were regarded as distinct but not architectonic foci."

is *primarily* in God's mind. Hittinger does acknowledge that it is also correct to consider natural law to be in the creature. "Insofar as natural law can be said to be 'in' things or nature, it is an order of inclinations of reason and will by which men are moved to the common good" (11). But his unusually strong theological emphasis remains regarding the natural law as law. Is natural law primarily in God or in created nature?

When Aquinas defines natural law, in q. 91, a. 2 of the *Prima Secundae*, he specifies that the natural law is a participation of the eternal law in the rational creature.[2] Clearly, if the natural law were not somehow in the creature it would be in no way distinct from the eternal law. While drawing from Stephen Brock's Thomistic study of qq. 91–93, Hittinger contends that natural law is not something diverse from the eternal law (xxi).[3] Although the two are distinguishable in our minds, the natural law is simply a participation of the eternal law.[4] In Aquinas's response to the second objection in q. 91, a. 2, his intent is to refute the objector's contention that there is no such thing as natural law. His point is to keep natural law from being entirely subsumed by the eternal law while, of course, holding that natural law is a participation in the eternal law. Aquinas's defense of the existence of natural law entails that it may be distinguished from the eternal law within our minds on account of real differences between the two, such as, where the two laws are located in reality. Since the two laws have a common source, to determine their location, and therefore their differences, it is necessary to consider the order between them.

Although the eternal law is first in the descending order of being, according to the ascending order of names, natural law is first in nature because, in the order of cognition, we first come to know that which is most evident to our creaturely minds. To come to know that we are governed by God's law we must first realize that we are governed. The human first discovers the good as a finite object of desire. Only later does the human come to discover that particular and partial goods are ordered among themselves and that they are themselves ordered to a higher and absolutely transcendent good. The primitive understanding of goods as not yet ordered to an absolutely higher one may be classified as practical knowledge. Although such primitive understanding qualifies as practical knowledge, it is not yet even close to wisdom and not yet sufficient for human action in the full sense described in Aquinas's teaching regarding the use of reason, the moral good, and the final end at *Summa Theologiae*, I-II, q. 89, a.

---

2   *ST*, I-II, q. 91, a. 2: "Unde patet quod lex naturalis nihil aliud est quam participatio legis aeternae in rationali creatura."

3   See Stephen Louis Brock, *The Legal Character of Natural Law According to St. Thomas Aquinas*, dissertation (Toronto: University of Toronto Press, 1988), ch. 2-C.

4   *ST*, I-II, q. 91, a. 2, ad 1: "Ad primum ergo dicendum quod ratio illa procederet, si lex naturalis esset aliquid diversum a lege aeterna. Non autem est nisi quaedam participatio eius."

6 or even in Aquinas's treatise on moral action earlier on in the *Prima Secundae* in qq. 6–21. In the order of knowing, to come to understand ourselves as subjects of divine law, we first realize that we are ordered to lower goods. Our being ordered to those lower goods is more evident to us than is our understanding of God as the universal Legislator and provident King responsible for the universal common good.

In his chapter "Natural Law as 'Law,'" Hittinger controversially affirms that according to John Paul II's reading of sacred Scripture, "there is not morality and then the law" (41). According to Hittinger, morality neither precedes law nor is separable from it. While that may very well be the case for the human race as the people of God in the history of salvation, and therefore coincides with recent papal interpretations of the fall in the Garden of Eden, according to which divine law precedes the human experience of morality, perhaps it is not an entirely accurate description of how individual humans come to know the moral law while relying on the power of natural reason. The first, seminal understanding, although still insufficient for fully human action, capacitates us to rationally direct ourselves so as to seek partial goods as ends.[5] Only later, although not much later, do we come to understand that, for the sake of attaining personal happiness, we are obliged to order ourselves and everything else to a single end.

In addition to the distinction between the order of knowing and the order of being, a more detailed distinction within the order of human knowing is helpful in the study of the primary location of natural law: namely, the distinction between spontaneous and scientific understanding. Insofar as scientific understanding reflects the causal order of things, the scientific knowledge of professional philosophers and theologians more closely approximates the order of being than the spontaneous understanding by which real human beings really come to know. Awareness of the specificities of scientific knowledge should prevent us from extending the peculiar features of the scholarly mind to the ordinary discovery of the common man. Consequently, even today, natural law theory ought to conserve the traditional appreciation for what comes first in the order of discovery, even if such primitive knowledge is not yet sufficient for perfect action, or even properly human, moral action.

In order to counter common modern moral philosophies with their view of

---

5   Regarding the full cognitive requirements for moral action and the difference between moral action and other rational activity in Aquinas, see, for instance, *ST*, I-II, q. 6, a. 1: "Et ideo, cum utrumque sit ab intrinseco principio, scilicet quod agunt, et quod propter finem agunt, horum motus et actus dicuntur voluntarii, hoc enim importat nomen voluntarii, quod motus et actus sit a propria inclinatione. Et inde est quod voluntarium dicitur esse, secundum definitionem Aristotelis et Gregorii Nysseni et Damasceni, non solum cuius principium est intra, sed cum additione scientiae. Unde, cum homo maxime cognoscat finem sui operis et moveat seipsum, in eius actibus maxime voluntarium invenitur."

an autonomous human reason, *The First Grace* continues its discussion of the relationship between morality and law by emphasizing how the human mind is always extrinsically regulated. In human action, rational deliberation must always take into consideration the reality of human possibilities and therefore the nature of both oneself and one's instruments. As human beings, in addition to our intrinsic inclination towards our not yet achieved final perfection, we are also regulated extrinsically by the divine Legislator on account of our participation in his eternal law. Hittinger remarks that "The notion of participation is restated in the context of *Gen.* 2: 17 in order to emphasize that the human mind is a measured measure, and that the first principle of its practical activity is its participation in a divinely given law. [...] the created intellect is not the first measure of the *bonum* and *malum*. [...] creatures share in, but do not constitute the measure of, moral good and evil" (41). Hittinger's emphasis on the measuring and regulating role of God could be difficult to reconcile with some particular texts of Aquinas, like q. 90, a. 1, ad 1, where Aquinas affirms that human reason itself is a rule and a measure in comparison to human actions which are measured and ruled.[6] In fact, it is even more difficult to reconcile with Aquinas, the negation included within Hittinger's claim later on in *The First Grace* that: "The human mind is a measured measure (*mensura mensurata*) not a measuring measure (*mensura mensurans*)" (97). Every measure must somehow measure. Perhaps here Hittinger simply exaggerates his point regarding the divine dependency of human reason as a reaction against those scholars who exclude the theonomic character of natural law as a component necessary for it to be understood as law. As an alternative to Hittinger's proposal, the divine origin of natural law may be emphasized without subtracting from its natural, rational, and creaturely character. Indeed, although Aquinas might not appreciate the redundant terminology, perhaps he would agree with the proposition that the human mind is a *mensura mensurans mensurata*, a measured and measuring measure.

Despite the landmark work of scholars such as Jacques Maritain and Servais Pinckaers in overcoming legalistic interpretations, unfortunately, many still read the *Treatise on Law* out of its context within the whole of the *Summa Theologiae*. If one studies the *Treatise on Law* as though it were a book all on its own, one can notice Aquinas repeating that reason is the rule for human action but miss the following important point illustrated by Hittinger's

6   *ST*, I-II, q. 90, a. 1, ad 1: "Ad primum ergo dicendum quod, cum lex sit regula quaedam et mensura, dicitur dupliciter esse in aliquo. Uno modo, sicut in mensurante et regulante. Et quia hoc est proprium rationis, ideo per hunc modum lex est in ratione sola. Alio modo, sicut in regulato et mensurato. Et sic lex est in omnibus quae inclinantur in aliquid ex aliqua lege, ita quod quaelibet inclinatio proveniens ex aliqua lege, potest dici lex, non essentialiter, sed quasi participative. Et hoc modo inclinatio ipsa membrorum ad concupiscendum lex membrorum vocatur."

development of "participated theonomy." Moral reason is indeed a rule and measure of human action but only because and insofar as it is ruled by God.[7]

Allow me to conclude this first topic regarding the relationship between the eternal law in God and the natural law in human nature, with a modest proposal. Although *The First Grace* offers a crucial contribution to contemporary scholarship on natural law by emphasizing its theonomic character, a few of its bolder claims might acquire even greater persuasive force by adding the nuance needed to maintain greater respect for the specifically natural character of natural law.

Hittinger has helped clarify that knowledge required for full human action and the scientific understanding of the natural law must include the recognition of natural law's causal origin in God. Nonetheless, such recognition of its divine origin does not exclude that the natural law, while being from God and inscribed by God, is inscribed by God precisely in human nature. Human reason judges and directs but never just on its own authority. The most particular prudential *dictamen* is authoritative insofar as it is a participation in the divine light. In the practical order of moral action, right reason is both reasonable and authoritative, both internal and external in its source of directive power. As Aquinas writes in q. 94, the central question for his theory of natural law, natural law is a kind of knowledge, even a work of reason, *opus rationis*.[8] He compares how natural law is constituted by reason to how a proposition is also constituted by reason. The knowledge needed to be subjects of natural law according to our human nature requires and includes the recognition that every moral exigency is at once for the good of our nature and willed by God for our good in accord with his omniscience.

Now I will turn to an issue of particular importance for ecumenical dialogue: the relationship between nature and grace in Hittinger's description of natural law. Regarding the historical paradigm of natural law within the context of the history of salvation, Hittinger contends that the "time of natural law," that is, the historical and moral condition from Adam to Moses, "is not normative for Thomas's ethics. And [...] the effort to *make* that condition normative marks the modern project" (11). Although Hittinger's terminology may seem curious, if not eccentric, even to some Thomists, to call a historical period as "of natural law," coincides perfectly with Thomas's own usage.[9] By warning us not to view

---

7   Regarding law's presence in human reason, Hittinger develops the topic further but in an entirely different context and without adding nuance to his former claims about natural law being in God's mind, see 95–96.

8   See *ST*, I-II, 94, a. 1: "lex naturalis est aliquid per rationem constitutum, sicut etiam propositio est quoddam opus rationis."

9   See, for example, *ST*, I-II, q. 98, a. 6: "Et ideo inter legem naturae et legem gratiae, oportuit legem veterem dari."

the "time of natural law" as paradigmatic for the shaping of natural law theory, Hittinger means that we ought not to look to the condition of humankind, without the aid of the preternatural gifts and without the assistance of either the Mosaic or the Christian divine positive law, in the historical period from Adam to Moses as the paradigmatic period of natural law or as the human condition properly considered by moral philosophy. Hittinger rightly emphasizes that, for Aquinas, fulfillment of natural law requires belonging to a community of virtue and the supernatural aid of sanctifying grace.

Hittinger's focus on natural law within the fullness of revelation offers important insight towards the recovery of a full comprehension of Aquinas's theory of natural law. Nevertheless, the historical period from Adam to Moses is most relevant for distinguishing between the demands that are proper to human nature according to the order of creation and those demands that are specific to biblical revelation and the economy of salvation. This careful distinction, but of course not the separation, between these two complementary sets of demands, those of nature and those of biblical revelation, permits the theologian to better characterize the ironic pedagogy within God's instruction of his chosen people. Throughout the history of revelation, God providentially designed that his people might learn, again and again, through their own tragic failure, that their human, even natural, happiness is unattainable unless they faithfully turn to their divine Savior. The perverse tendencies of fallen nature were medicinally instilled in humankind along with the natural law in order to remind us of our need for salvation. While natural law points us in the right direction, the *fomes peccati* remind us of the insufficiency of our nature and of our nature's law for the attainment of human happiness.

Of course, by defending the use of the term "time of natural law" as an historical locus for a systematic thought experiment in order to distinguish between the natural and the supernatural within us, I do not mean to imply that the demands proper to natural law may be known better without the aid of grace or without the instruction specific to the divine positive law afforded us by the Mosaic Law and by Christian revelation. Nor do I mean to imply that anyone could fulfill the natural law without also being under the New Law of the Holy Spirit. Indeed, for Aquinas, no one can fulfill the natural law without also enjoying the benefits of the new. For all the children of Adam and Eve, fulfillment of the natural law requires the aid of divine grace. Aquinas affirms that throughout all of history, including the time after Adam and prior to Moses, there were those who lived under the New Law on account of their fulfillment of natural law, as indicated by St. Paul in *Romans* 2: 14, and on account of their faith and hope in a Messiah or remunerator who would come.[10] Moreover, for Aquinas,

---

10   See, for instance, *ST*, I-II, q. 106, a. 3, ad 2: "omni tempore fuerint aliqui ad novum testamentum pertinentes, ut supra dictum est." See also: 1 *Tim.*, 2, 4, Revised

because of the effects of original sin, no human can act for his due end without enjoying the justification of saving grace.[11] Even those who lived before the Incarnation can only respect the natural law with the aid offered by Christ. In the case of those who lived before the Incarnation, his aid is offered in anticipation of the redemption which he won through the paschal mysteries of his suffering, death, and resurrection. Although the fulfillment of the natural law and the New Law are existentially inseparable, their careful distinction can lead to a better understanding of both. By examining the existential condition of those who lived in the so-called "time of natural law," the Thomist can find the criteria needed to distinguish between the demands of nature and those of divine positive law. In contrast, by excluding consideration of the historical "time of natural law," the Thomist cannot develop a balanced understanding of the relationship between the natural, the Old, and the New Law, and therefore, between nature and grace.

Even if the study of the "time of natural law" is, of itself, more interesting for the theologian than for the political philosopher, Hittinger has made such a strong case for the need to take into account the theological presuppositions of natural law, that no proponent of natural law, even a lawyer or political scientist, should now remain indifferent to this topic in its relation to the other times of history because of its usefulness for determining the requirements for the fulfillment of the natural law as a demand, not just of nature, but also of God.

Regarding the relationship between nature and grace in Thomistic natural law theory, Hittinger emphasizes that salvific grace is necessary for the fulfillment of natural law. For Hittinger, it would be Pelagian to interpret *Romans* 2: 14 to imply that the pagans could fulfill parts of the law without the aid of reforming and redemptive grace (10). The created order is so bent by sin that movement in accord with nature "requires the remediation of divine positive law and a new law of grace" (11). And, while drawing from Pope John Paul II's encyclical *Veritatis Splendor*, Hittinger contends that "human reason, endeavoring to construct the conditions for human fulfillment, needs revelation and grace" (32). Moreover, according to Hittinger, "the modern, secular construction of natural law is contrary to the Gospel [...] [and] as destructive within the house of Catholic moral theology as it was in the Protestant denominations" (33).

Clearly, in order to sort out these issues regarding nature and grace in the fulfillment of human nature, much depends on the anthropology and theology

---

Standard Version *(RSV):* "Who desires all men to be saved and to come to the knowledge of the truth." And: *Heb.* 11, 6 *(RSV)*: "And without faith it is impossible to please him. For whoever would draw near to God must believe that he exists and that he rewards those who seek him."

11   See, for example, *ST*, I-II, q. 89, a. 6.

that Hittinger affirmed must be clarified in order that natural law theory may be effectively advanced in our post-Christian world. Nonetheless, despite the energy and extension dedicated to analyzing the rational need for scientific understanding to recognize the divine source of natural law, *The First Grace* does not offer a detailed description of the human requirements for receiving the gift of the New Law so as to be able to fulfill the natural law. Hittinger criticizes Suarez's interpretation of Thomas regarding the requirements for the promulgation of natural law but does not offer a detailed and satisfying theory of his own (51–57).

Several important questions remain and *The First Grace* renders them even more pressing. What must the human being understand regarding the source of natural law in order to be a rational subject of that law? What difference is there between acting according to one's recognition of God as the source of the law naturally known by the mind or hoping in a superhuman remunerator? To put the question more succinctly, what naturally obtained knowledge of the divine legislator is needed for the human being to be properly subject to natural law and how does such natural knowledge differ from the faith-inspired understanding of the Redeemer? Surely, Russell Hittinger did not promise to answer these extremely difficult questions and a good case can be made for their being outside the scope of this book. And yet they are so deeply related to the issues examined in *The First Grace* that it would seem that these questions regarding supernatural anthropology need to be resolved in order to effectively advance our understanding of natural law, both within the Church and without. Hittinger notes that the ultimate source of natural law's authority has been avoided or ignored by many scholars because: "Among secular philosophers and jurists, the theological question became burdensome, especially in political, legal, and professional discourse that has no stake in, or even rejects, the possibility of consensus about matters theological" (62). But the rational recovery of natural law requires addressing the issue of its source of authority and therefore resolving the more urgent questions regarding natural law's relationship with the eternal law.

I entitled my commentary with the question, *"Grace or Nature First?"* Perhaps Hittinger would agree that, in the order of being, God's gift is first, and also last; while in the order of knowing, our understanding of natural law must first begin with nature, even though it is only under the New Law, as children of God, that we can fully understand the moral exigencies of our nature.

Religious Freedom, State Neutrality, and Divine Authority

Matthew Levering

Commenting upon *Dignitatis Humanae*, Russell Hittinger points out, "It may prove surprising, if not frustrating, that *DH* puts to one side theoretical treatment of the issues that directly touch, in American terms, upon establishment of religion. . . . For the Second Vatican Council, it was quite enough to tackle the problem of the religious civil liberties of individuals, communities, and the Church herself." Hittinger's book, however, signals that this approach is no longer enough.

Let me first summarize Hittinger's book. After briefly developing an account of natural law in itself (the first two chapters), which I will describe more fully below, *The First Grace* focuses upon the role of the judiciary, specifically that of the United States, *vis-à-vis* natural law (chapters three through eight). Here Hittinger argues that discerning and encoding the natural law (in positive law) is a task that belongs to legislators, but that in the twentieth century this legislative task has been usurped in the United States by the judiciary, particularly the Supreme Court. As Hittinger shows, in case after case (post-World War II), the Court has identified the natural law with rights that originate in the individual, understood as radically autonomous from social bonds. Hittinger suggests that reversing the Court's usurpation of authority depends upon the development of public awareness of a constitutional crisis, similar to that caused by Dred Scott.

The final three chapters of the book contextualize the new understanding of natural law as undergirding radical autonomy. Chapters nine and eleven address the issue in terms of the relationship of Church and state, while chapter ten explores the development of liberalism itself. Importantly, chapter nine shows that this understanding of the radical autonomy of individuals is not ratified by *Dignitatis Humanae*, as some theologians, overreading the document, have argued. Hittinger shows that *Dignitatis Humanae* defends religious freedom without taking up the broader topic of Church-state relations. Chapter ten then offers a nuanced exploration of the roots of the contemporary situation in liberal romanticism's ideal of the individual genius, including the individual religious genius, as the engine of cultural development. Following Christopher Dawson, Hittinger suggests that the radically autonomous individual marks the triumph of consumerist *techne* over against the Victorian Enlightenment's valuation of familial, economic, and political bonds. A radical autonomy fostered by technology represents a vulgarization, in Dawson's view, of the Victorian liberal ideal of the role of the autonomous genius as the formative mediator of culture and of religious experience.

Finally, chapter eleven argues in agreement with Jacques Maritain that the answer is not to return to sacral conceptions of the state, in which the state embodies the temporal common good, in union with the Church as the embodiment of the supernatural common good. For Maritain, along with Popes Pius XII and John Paul II, the "body politic" is not reducible to the state. Instead, the state instrumentally serves the common good by fostering the various societies that compose the body politic. The danger of this view of the state, a danger exemplified by the work of Ernest Gellner, is that once one conceives the state in instrumentalist terms, it becomes difficult to conceive of any society, or societies, ordered to a higher, non-instrumental end. In Aquinas's defense of the mendicant orders, Hittinger finds a way of defending the existence of various societies, ordered to the common good, within the body politic.

Reading Hittinger's book can lead to a profound state of demoralization. Mustering superb erudition and eloquence, he demonstrates that law in Western societies has entered into a dreadful and far-reaching morass. One is inclined to ask the old Russian question, "How then should we live?" Is there anything that can be done to improve the situation?

In my view, Hittinger's work leads toward the answer that the Church, once again, needs to develop her understanding of her relation to states. We might begin by examining more closely Hittinger's teaching on natural law, especially in his first chapter. From his study of Aquinas, Hittinger notes that natural law is located in three "foci": the human mind, nature, and the mind of God. The former two, Hittinger shows, depend upon the latter. As law, the natural law is in the mind of God. In a participated way, the natural law is in human minds (as first principles) and in nature (the providential order). Thus, without recognizing the relation of the created order to the Creator, it is impossible to develop an adequate account of "natural law."

Why is this so? Could not human beings simply recognize first principles, or recognize the order of nature, without ever adverting to the question of God? The answer is no, for two reasons. First, Hittinger points out that "[n]atural law is never (and I must emphasize never) defined in terms of what is first in the (human) mind or first in nature." Were one to avoid the question of God, one could not define natural law, since natural law requires a lawgiver to be law. As

Hittinger shows, "Without the order of priority, we have either nature or the human mind as the cause of the law – not the cause of knowing or discovering, but the cause of the law itself." In both cases, God would be an enemy of the autonomous authority of the "natural law." Furthermore, if nature is the cause, then the natural law seems to be opposed, in Cartesian fashion, to human (rational) freedom; if the human mind is the cause, then the natural law seems to be, at bottom, a human construct (whether articulated in secular positive law or in the laws promulgated by the Church's Magisterium). As Hittinger states, "When the starting points are made autonomous, the human mind declares independence not only from the deeper order of divine tutoring but also from the tutoring afforded by human culture, including human law." Thus by avoiding the question of God, one turns the natural law into its opposite. The natural law becomes variously indicative of *human autonomy*, whereas in fact the natural law is *participated theonomy*, in Pope John Paul II's phrase from *Veritatis Splendor*.

The second reason for the impossibility of separating the natural law from the order of divine providence is not unrelated to the first. Hittinger sets himself apart from some philosophers, though not from Aquinas, by taking sin seriously. Summarizing Aquinas's position, he argues that human beings cannot simply recognize the mind's first principles or the order of nature, since turning away from God distorts the human ability to make judgments about the precepts of the natural law:

"As a law, natural law is not 'in' nature or the human mind, but is rather in the mind of God. The immutability of natural law, he insists, is due to the 'immutability and perfection of the divine reason that institutes it.' Insofar as natural law can be said to be 'in' things or nature, it is an order of inclinations of reason and will by which men are moved to a common good. While the created order continues to move men, the effect of that law (in the creature) is bent by sin – not so bent that God fails to move the finite mind, for the fallen man is still a spiritual creature, possessed of the God-given light of moral understanding, but bent enough that this movement requires the remediation of divine positive law and a new law of grace."

Hittinger goes on to remark that whereas Aquinas does not envision resolving ethical problems solely from the perspective of the natural law abstracted from theology (natural or revealed), modern theorists of the natural law have sought to do so, with results that evidence the necessity of the "remediation of divine positive law and a new law of grace." This modern conception of natural law represents a break, Hittinger demonstrates, with the development of natural law doctrine from at least the 2nd century A.D., a legal tradition from which the Protestant Reformers did not dissent. The break occurs with the Enlightenment thinkers, Hobbes, Locke, Rousseau, and Kant.

How then might one go about restoring the priority of divine providence in the conception of natural law? Hittinger argues that the autonomous view of natural law has so distorted the concept that employing it in public discourse is counter-productive. He writes, "It seems to me that the expression 'natural law' ought to be avoided whenever possible in the Christian address to the world about worldly things." Instead, in order to express the meaning of "natural law," he suggests using the phrase "higher law," which has been used in important ways by American public intellectuals over America's history. Hittinger also proposes paying deeper attention to two of Pope John Paul II's recent encyclicals, *Veritatis Splendor* and *Evangelium Vitae*. Regarding the latter encyclical, he notes that "the Pope vigorously supports the modern experiment in constitutional democracy and human rights. But once he discerned that the rhetoric of natural rights was being used to justify killing the unborn and infirm, he took his readers in *Evangelium Vitae* back to the book of Genesis." The first chapters of Genesis display how human rationality and morality are inscribed within the order of divine providence. *Evangelium Vitae* aims at renewing public discourse; *Veritatis Splendor*, in contrast, works to renew the Church's theology by reintegrating "natural law into the dogmatic theology of revelation and Christology."

But are these two encyclicals enough of a solution? Without disagreeing with the substance of his ideas and proposals, one may reasonably doubt that even Hittinger thinks so. The Pope's superb efforts in *Evangelium Vitae* and *Veritatis Splendor* to recover, among other things, the foundations for proper natural law discourse need to be considered in light of what we learn in the concluding chapters, nine through eleven, of *The First Grace*. In these chapters, as we recall, Hittinger discusses, respectively, *Dignitatis Humanae* in light of its self-imposed limitation to the problem of religious liberty; Christopher Dawson's theory of the vulgarization of the romantic ideal of the genius in the radical autonomy embedded in consumerist technology; and the difficulty in preserving the notions of solidarity or the common good (i.e., the idea of a unified, non-instrumental telos) once the state is conceived as an instrument fostering the particular goods of the various societies that constitute the body politic.

The central issue might be phrased as follows. First, atomistic pluralism has been generated by understanding the state as a limited rather than absolute temporal entity, despite the gains made by such an understanding. Second, the pretense to radical autonomy is intrinsic to a technology-driven economy and culture. Third, these two stimulants of radical autonomy work together: the state often serves the needs of the technology-driven economy, and the formation of citizens within this culture shapes the state's own conception of citizenship. How should theologians, and the Church, respond to this situation?

I think that Hittinger's book presses toward an answer that goes beyond *Evangelium Vitae* and *Veritatis Splendor*, important as they are, and implicitly calls for a development of *Dignitatis Humanae*. As Hittinger points out, the Church in *Dignitatis Humanae* does not advance a neutral conception of freedom.

Rather, the "freedom" that the Church claims for herself has its roots in her mission from Christ to bring the blessings of salvation to the world. This raises two questions that bear upon the situation sketched by Hittinger. First, can states recognize the "freedom" that the Church claims for herself, without recognizing the source of such "freedom"? Is it really possible for a state to remain neutral over time about the identity of God, and continue to recognize a "freedom" that is only understandable in light of a claim to a transcendent source? Second, if states simply remain neutral, can states avoid granting eventually that one god is as good as another? Would this not mean that states would eventually grant the notion that "gods" are constructs – technological products – selected and consumed by autonomous individuals with diverse and equally acceptable ends in view?

Depending upon one's answers to those two questions, one might be led to deny that a viable notion of "higher law" or "common good" is actually possible without a state that concretely, and not merely by (easily deconstructed) deist residues, confesses God. Certainly, the example of the United States, and also of the European Union and Canada, suggests that even a large amount of deist, and even Judeo-Christian, residue, cannot hold out against the forces of radical autonomy for very long.

It seems to me, in short, that the conception of natural law rightly required by Hittinger cannot be (re)gained without further exploration of "the question of whether the state should somehow manifest or exemplify the claims of the one true Church." At least, such questions appear to be the direction in which Hittinger's work leads.

Natural Law Argument in a Post-Christian World (Or, Why Catholic Moralists need the Agrarians, and Vice Versa)

Joshua P. Hochschild

Professor Hittinger's book touches on a cornucopia of issues surrounding natural law – questions of moral and social theology, history, jurisprudence, and constitutional theory and practice. I want to reflect on the significance of the fact that, despite all this, the book does not really contain any *natural law arguments*. This is a slight exaggeration, but only a very slight one;[1] in any case, the book does not take up natural law arguments as its primary concern. By a natural law argument, I mean a moral argument that appeals to natural law in defense of a particular moral position, the kind of argument that might move, say, from premises about the nature and good of man to conclusions about the evil of abortion or euthanasia, or the good of marriage; or from premises about the nature and good of marriage to a conclusion about the evil of divorce or contraception. Although it is clear where Professor Hittinger stands on the moral status of such things as abortion, euthanasia, and contraception, and one may be able to reconstruct from the book the outline of natural law arguments for these positions, the book is not concerned to make such arguments.

This observation is certainly not a criticism of the book. In fact, appropriately enough, most scholarly books on natural law today tend to be weighted heavily toward meta-ethical concerns. Hittinger himself has made a considered and deliberate choice to de-emphasize particular natural law arguments, with a rationale summarized in the final paragraph of his "Introduction":

> The problem of natural law cannot be understood adequately as an argumentative exercise pointing to, or issuing from, moral premises. Such an exercise is important, but it does not touch and therefore cannot resolve the deeper issue of the original situation of human practical reason. When the Pope's commission of moral theologians argued for the priority of a human

---

1   As Hittinger points out in response to these remarks, the argument of Ch. 4 about the authority to render judgment is a natural law argument.

dominion in which human practical reason supplies the concrete norms,[2] or
when the Supreme Court declared in *Casey* that the individual has natural
immunity from positive law in the matter of abortion, it is important to
understand that these are not moral arguments but claims about what is
prior to arguments. The answer to this question is entirely relevant to
morals, but nothing in the logic of moral argument *per se* can win the case.
The question turns upon considerations of anthropology and theology. To
attempt to rediscover the natural law in a post-Christian world we must pick
up the discussion precisely at this point (xlv–xlvi).

In short, the kinds of challenges faced by proponents of natural law today
cannot be met on the level of the moral arguments, but must be met on prior
ground; theological and anthropological questions thus take strategic prece-
dence over moral questions. This is a position – which I find entirely agreeable
– which makes it appropriate for Hittinger to address the issue of natural law in
the context of such a wide range of questions – questions of political theory,
jurisprudence, constitutional theory and history, Catholic moral theology, etc.,
for in all of these contexts emerge the crucial anthropological and theological
questions which must be raised in the project of "rediscovering" a proper sense
of the natural law.

Hittinger's focus on anthropology and theology might make it seem as if he
views the project of "rediscovering natural law" as primarily a philosophical
one, but in fact he is conscious that it is a cultural problem as well. The challenge is not just a matter of theory, but one which is at the heart of the "culture-
forming mission of Christianity." This is another reason why it is appropriate
that Hittinger touches on so many different issues in his book; it is not simply
that he is trying to cover his bases philosophically, but that he is trying to show
the practical relevance of these ideas "all the way down," not only in the debates
of moral theologians but in the drama of political decisions and historical developments, in the daily lives of judges and citizens, in the details of how we perceive the world and our place in it. The project of rediscovering the natural law
is not just a matter of theoretical argumentation, but of cultural evangelization.

But what could be the role for *natural law arguments* in this project? In the
long passage quoted above, Hittinger agrees that the natural law argument,
"moral argument," is "important." But how, and in what sense? While I agree
that "nothing in the logic of moral argument *per se* can win the case" about the
relevant theological and anthropological issues that are at stake, it seems to me
that there is something in the exercise of such argument that *can* be of essential
help in winning the case.

In raising the question of the role of natural law arguments, I am aware that

---

2   Hittinger has in mind an unfortunate and happily ignored 1967 report on contracep-
     tion presented to Paul VI, discussed by Hittinger on pp. xliv–xlv.

many today hold that they have no place in public discourse. Hittinger would not agree, although he has his warnings about the public use of natural law argument. He warns us not to *depend* on the moral arguments, neglecting the theological and anthropological questions. He also suggests that the use of the very term "natural law" "ought to be avoided whenever possible in the Christian address to the world about worldly things," (34) since for a variety of reasons the term is misleading (Hittinger suggests the alternative "higher law"). But of course neither of these are recommendations against the use of natural law arguments in public discourse; they are recommendation about dialectical and rhetorical strategy.

More importantly, Hittinger fears that too many people today have "the impression that talk about natural law is a rhetoric designed to achieve consensus about matters of public policy" (16). Natural law arguments are supposed to achieve this consensus by appealing to what is universally known, which, Hittinger fears, involves "trimming arguments to fit what is first in cognition" (17). Of course some people also have another impression, that natural law arguments are supposed to lead to "conclusions grounded in Church authority" (16). The result is a doubly misleading impression, with natural law

> placed in the most unfortunate position of being organized around two extreme poles. On the one end, it represented the conclusions of church authority; on the other end, it represented what every agent is supposed to know according to what is first in cognition. We have Cartesian minds somehow under church discipline (21).

But does any of this entail that natural law arguments have no place in public discourse? I don't think so, and neither does Hittinger. Hittinger is reminding us that natural law arguments should not be expected to be persuasive in themselves, not only because they cannot satisfy the strict liberal standards of "public reason," but because even apart from those standards they just don't happen to be rhetorically effective for a "post-Christian" audience.

But why aren't they effective? In large part because such arguments must appeal to premises which themselves fail to achieve consensus – the anthropological and theological premises to which Hittinger turns our attention. But why do the premises of natural law arguments fail to secure universal assent? There are those who would argue that the failure to secure universal assent is evidence that there is no such thing as natural law. Of course classical examples of universalistic morals always include accounts of why some people *happen* to fail to know what is *in principle* available to everyone; the grasp of moral truths in principle available to anyone may not be in fact available to those who are poorly educated (e.g. Plato's *Republic*) or especially disobedient to God (e.g. *Romans* 1). Indeed one could even say that it is a precondition of any good natural law theory that it include the resources for accounting for the conditions of its failure to achieve consensus; and I am inclined to agree with Alasdair

MacIntyre who, in explicitly taking up this challenge, has argued that Thomistic natural law theory does account for the precise sort of failure to appreciate natural law exhibited by "the dominant cultures of advanced modernity."[3]

MacIntyre, much like Hittinger, blames the failure of natural law arguments today partly on bad theory, especially bad anthropology: a corrupted notion of "choice" and its role in moral agency. But the mistaken anthropology is, for most people, neither explicit nor the fruit of theorizing; it is implicit in corrupt practice. Thus MacIntyre points to sociological or cultural factors that contribute to the failure. We can summarize these factors roughly in terms of "the great transformation"[4] of economic life of which the "dominant culture of advanced modernity" is the fruit. Renowned as a critic of liberalism, we must remember that MacIntyre sometimes seems to regard liberal ideas as epiphenomena of technological, industrial society; whatever else has changed, MacIntyre is ever the critic of capitalism, the tone of this criticism simply evolving from Trotskyite[5] to agrarian.[6]

I perceive the agrarian spirit in Hittinger too, especially in the last two essays of the volume: first, in the context of his review of Christopher Dawson's criticism of technology (Ch. 10, "Technology and the Demise of Liberalism"), and second, in his discussion of the liberal instrumentalist view of civil society, especially as this tends to violate the principle of subsidiarity (Ch. 11, "Reasons for Civil Society"). In the former chapter, Hittinger describes Dawson's argument that secularism is to be blamed more on technologism than liberalism. "Real secularism, according to Dawson, could not emerge until technology made it possible for most people to live without the ideals and practices of the older Western order" (251). The point isn't just that technology is anti-traditional, helping people do new things and break from old ways; but rather that the things that technology claims to do for us were once done by other means, namely by particular kinds of common activities, and these activities were

---

3   MacIntyre, "Theories of Natural Law in the Culture of Advanced Modernity," in *Common Truths: New Perspectives in Natural Law*, ed. Edward B. McLean (Wilmington, Delaware: ISI Books, 2000) 91–115.

4   Karl Polanyi's phrase; MacIntyre calls Polanyi's *The Great Transoformation* (1944) "still the single most illuminating account of the inception of institutionalized modernity." *Whose Justice? Which Rationality?* (Notre Dame: University of Notre Dame Press, 1988), 211. Cf. *After Virtue* (Notre Dame: University of Notre Dame Press, 1981) 239.

5   Cf. *After Virtue*, ch. 18, where the ingredients of MacIntyre's position are "Aristotle, Trotsky, and St. Benedict."

6   Cf. "Politics, Philosophy and the Common Good," in *The MacIntyre Reader* (Notre Dame: University of Notre Dame Press, 1998) 235–252, where MacIntyre suggests that Aristotle needs to be corrected in light of the agrarian tradition (250–251). And already MacIntyre was taking cues from Cobbett's *Rural Rides* in *After Virtue*, 238–239.

regarded, by those who participated in them, as not only instrumental goods, but as having goods intrinsic to them.

Secularism, thus understood, involves an instrumentalist view of culture; thus it is essentially linked to pervasive and powerful technology because it involves

> the systematic application of tools to culture, especially to those areas of culture which had always been reproduced by humanistic activity, for example, sexual intercourse, family, religion, economic exchange. In short, by technology, Dawson meant the practice(s) of treating culture in the same way that the tool treats the natural environment. And this is simply another way of saying that the tool is no longer an instrument but rather the measure of the human world (251).

This critique – Dawson's, and presumably Hittinger's – is a cultural critique. The criticism, Hittinger explains, "is not aimed at the tool per se." It has

> nothing to do with the older and, in our context, misleading notion of 'labor-saving' devices. Rather it is aimed at a new cultural pattern in which tools are either deliberately designed to replace the human act or at least have the unintended effect of making the human act unnecessary or subordinate to the machine (252).

The problem then, is not technology itself, but technological culture, a culture in which the machine "promises an activity superior to the human act"(264).

I find the distinction between tool as labor-saving device and tool as replacement for the human act useful and important, although I can anticipate an objection: that the distinction can be applied arbitrarily. A husband and wife who wanted to limit their number of children could engage in the work of NFP, or they could save themselves the trouble and contracept. Presumably Hittinger wants to say that the contraceptive pill, for instance, is not merely a labor-saving device (in more than one sense!), but a replacement of human activity which naturally belongs to marriage (and exercises such virtues as chastity, generosity, humility, to name a few). By contrast, say, most of us would probably think of a tractor or a car as just a labor-saving device. On the other hand, I imagine that the Amish position, for instance, is that the tractor and automobile are not just a labor-saving devices, but replacements for human acts, indeed whole networks of human acts (which exercise such virtues as patience, humility, peacefulness, frugality, health, not to mention what MacIntyre would call the "virtues of acknowledged dependence," which are so essential to "the politics of small-scale community"). On what basis could we disagree with the Amish about this? Perhaps this is why the critique of technological society always ends up sounding agrarian, for Heidegger[7] and MacIntyre as much as Dawson and Hittinger. Hittinger says that in modern technological society "the machine reorganizes and to some extent supplants the world of human action, in the moral sense of the term." What prevents him from mentioning factories, tractors, and automobiles in his list of examples of virtue-supplanting technologies: "the policy of mutually assured destruction supplants diplomacy; the contraceptive pill supplants chastity; the cinema supplants recreation, especially prayer; managerial and propaganda techniques replace older practices of virtue and loyalty, and so on" (251–252). Throw out the radio and take down the fiddle from the wall, Andrew Lytle once said. So the line between *labor-saving* and *act-replacing/virtue-supplanting* is a line we should all want to draw, but how and where can we draw it? In any case, it does not seem to me satisfactory to say that whether a technology counts as labor-saving or act-replacing is culturally dependent, if the distinction was itself meant to help us determine the difference between a healthy culture and an unhealthy one.

But if this is an objection to the idea that the distinction can be easily applied in practice, it is not an objection to the distinction itself, which is, as I have said, at least theoretically very important. It is, for instance, important for making any sense of two key notions in Catholic social teaching, the complementary principles of solidarity and subsidiarity. Subsidiarity is a principle that has been articulated only after the ideal it expresses began to erode. The idea is that various social functions belong properly to certain levels or spheres of human activity, and that the usurpation of those functions by higher or less local levels of association is an injustice, a violation of the principle of subsidiarity. Although often invoked as a principle meant to limit government, of course market forces can also tend to violate the principle of subsidiarity, tempting individuals, families, and communities to, as Hittinger says, "subcontract" or "outsource" their functions to other agents.[8] Clearly the very sense of the principle of subsidiarity, then, depends on the notion that different social associations have proper functions, that certain kinds of activities naturally belong to those associations. The challenge in articulating the principle of subsidiarity is that the kinds of widespread, wholesale social transformations made possible by technology and markets make it harder and harder to maintain that certain forms of social association are in fact any more natural or proper than others.

---

7   "The earth now reveals itself as a coal mining district, the soil as a mineral deposit. The field that the peasant formerly cultivated and set in order appears different from how it did when to set in order still meant to take care of and maintain. The work of the peasant does not challenge the soil of the field. In sowing grain it places seed in the keeping of the forces of growth and watches over its increase. But meanwhile even the cultivation of the field has come under the grip of another kind of setting-in-order, which *sets upon* nature. It sets upon it in the sense of challenging it. Agriculture is now the mechanized food industry." Martin Heidegger, "The Question Concerning Technology," trans. William Lovitt, in *Basic Writings* (New York: Harper and Row, 1977), 296.

8   On the tendency of markets to violate the principle of subsidiarity, cf. Joshua P. Hochschild, "The Principle of Subsidiarity and the Agrarian Ideal," in *Faith,*

It seems to me that Hittinger points to a helpful strategy here, which is to articulate the naturalness of associations and activities in terms of their *intrinsic values*. As he describes in his final chapter, "where collaboration is not an inherent, but a merely useful good, the grounds for subsidiarity are greatly weakened. Except on contingent grounds of efficiency, there is no good reason why the state should do everything, or by the same token, do nothing. Therefore, *it seems that a truly useful concept of subsidiarity depends upon a concept of solidarity that preserves the intrinsic value of collaborative activity*" (279, emphasis added). Thus, "It is only when we identify goods of common activities that we can discover a principled limit to the power of the state as well as to the subcontracting (or "outsourcing") mentality characteristic of markets." (280)

So while the usefulness of the principle of subsidiarity clearly depends on the notion that some forms of social arrangement are "natural," this naturalness must be expressed in terms of *value*, in particular, of the intrinsic value of certain common activities. I think this language could help to clarify certain natural law arguments. For example: One might mistakenly think that the Church's position on contraception is based on an *instrumental* view of the marriage relationship, and that only the *contracepting* couple is enjoying and valuing the consummation of marriage "for its own sake" and not as a means for the end of procreation. The best response on the Church's part is probably not to reinforce this impression and merely insist that the "nature" of marriage is such that its purpose is procreation. Rather, the Church must go further and argue that there is something inherently valuable, and not merely instrumental, in the marital act's procreative aspect. It seems to me that this is in fact the strategy of those encyclicals which argue for the essential link between the unitive and procreative dimensions of the marital act (*Humanae Vitae* and *Evangelium Vitae*; cf. *Casti Connubii*). These encyclicals argue that this link is not merely *instrumental* (it is not just something useful for heterosexual couples, so that they have an easier time acquiring children when they want to), but it is *valuable in its own sake*; and indeed we can go further and argue that *the collaborative activities* of husband and wife *in response* to that link are not merely instrumental, but are intrinsically valuable, as conditions of some of the virtues proper to marriage.

But now, to step back from this example and review where we have been: why do natural law arguments tend to be unpersuasive to a post-Christian audience? Because such an audience does not view certain forms of association as "natural." Why do they not view them as natural? Because they do not appreciate their *intrinsic value* but regard them as having at best only *instrumental value*, value that can, in principle, be accomplished by some other instrument. So, how can we persuade people that certain activities or practices are inherently valuable? As I see it, the two basic strategies are *narrative* and *argument*.

Morality, and Civil Society, ed. Dale McConkey and Peter Augustine Lawler (Lanham, Maryland: Lexington Books, 2003), pp. 41–68. Reprinted in *Faith and Reason* 27 (2002): 117–155.

The first strategy appeals to imagination and memory, through history, fiction, poetry, even the media of popular culture. For those who may have experienced healthy forms of association and their intrinsic values, it is important to keep the memory of these experiences alive; for those, increasingly, who do not, the artist must work to bring before the imagination an alternative vision of social arrangement with its own intrinsic values. It is not surprising to me that the importance of memory and imagination has long been recognized in the agrarian tradition; and I think it is the ability to conjure an alternative vision of life in poetry, fiction, and artful non-fiction that accounts for the significance, and the widespread appeal, of the most important living agrarian figure, Wendell Berry, whose work has been appreciated by MacIntyre.[9]

The other strategy is argument. Now much of the appropriate argument must be, as Hittinger insists, not so much *moral* as *anthropological* and *theological*; and so much of the argument must also take place where anthropology and theology are relevant but would otherwise remain only implicit: in political theory, jurisprudence, law, constitutional interpretation. But I think there is also a place for moral argument in recovering the sense of the intrinsic value of certain activities and practices. Moral argument can play this role precisely because the anthropological and theological questions are implicit in them. But then for natural law arguments to play an effective role in evangelizing culture, we must think of them in their dialectical, rather than their apodictic, function. We must remember that in making an argument we may not intend simply to *use* concepts; we may intend rather to *elicit* concepts. We may offer an argument not just to achieve assent to a conclusion, by appealing to pre-existing concepts; but to illuminate new conceptual possibilities, by displaying new concepts at work in unfamiliar contexts. If natural law arguments alone cannot be expected to secure moral consensus by their intrinsic logic, they can exemplify the kind of reasoning that would be required for moral certainty.

To put this another way, in making arguments to a corrupt culture, we should be aware of what will be, for that culture, "first in cognition" – where I am using that phrase not to indicate Cartesian rationalist ambition, but Aristotelian dialectical pedagogy. Natural law arguments can play an important public role today, not in defending particular moral conclusions, but in exhibiting genuine practical reason at work, and proposing the possibility of forgotten values. In short, in a post-Christian world our intention for the public use of a natural law argument must be, not to end a debate, but to start a conversation. That kind of conversation can head down many paths; and happily, we can see much farther down those paths thanks to the illumination of *The First Grace*.

---

9   Cf. MacIntyre, "Politics, Philosophy and the Common Good," 237.

Natural Law Without God?

Michael P. Zuckert

The question posed by the overall topic of our symposium – "ethics without God?" – very much tempts me to respond with the answer H. L. Mencken once gave to a similarly theological question. He was asked whether he believed in infant baptism. "Yes," he said, "I definitely do. I've seen it done many times." And I suppose the same can be said about ethics.

But to give Mencken's easy answer in this context would be to beg the question, or a number of the questions raised by Russell Hittinger's new and provocative collection of essays. For one thing, his book raises a somewhat more precise question: "Natural Law without God?" Natural law, we might say, is a subset of the broader category "ethics," and the Menckenian answer to the broader question may not apply to the narrower one. As I understand Hittinger's position, in fact, he does wish to answer, "no", to the question of whether one can have natural law without God.

Moreover, while he grants the Menckenean answer to the broader question in a sense, it appears to me that he would not, in the final analysis, accept that either. In his volume's lead essay he affirms the possibility of moral discourse separate from "sermonics and catechetics" (35), presumably moral discourse in its terms independent of God. Such discourse appears to be independent of natural law as he understands it, but, speaking of Catholics, he states the belief that "it is the natural law that renders the gentiles amenable to the rudiments of moral discourse. [...] [We] believe that what the gentiles know is an effect of divine pedagogy, whether the gentiles know it or not" (35). (Consider also: "theologically considered, there is not morality, and then law," 41). Hittinger then sees the existence of natural law as the (perhaps, unacknowledged) ground for the possibility of all moral discourse, and since natural law cannot be without God, he would answer our larger question quite differently from my Menckeneanizing response. That Aristotle, say, could do ethics (as a science) and live ethically (as a human person) was possible because of the divinely ordained natural law.

Hittinger gives little explicit defense of his answer to the broader question – it is striking that he leaves it entirely in the realm of belief – and I will follow him in focusing my attention on the natural law. Of course, there is something a bit both rash and foolish in my joining issue with him on natural law in this company. Being neither a Catholic nor a Thomist, nor nearly so knowledgeable about those matters as everyone else on this panel, my bringing forward my thoughts on these topics is rather like offering to show Michael Jordan my jump shot. So, at the risk of appearing either pretentious, or foolish – or most likely both – let me proceed.

Hittinger's sub-title is "Rediscovering Natural Law in a Post-Christian Era," but that can be misleading as to the character of his argument. His point is actually that we cannot get by with a "post-Christian" view of natural law; we need to recapture Christian, more precisely Thomistic natural law in this post-Christian era. Indeed, his account of natural law is nestled within a broader story of the history of natural law thinking; the Greeks were not really natural law thinkers; although there were a handful of references to natural law in pre-Christian days, the dominant Greek view was captured in the opposition they regularly saw between nature (physis) and law (nomos). "Natural law" was, for the Greeks, nearly an oxymoron (xix). The reflection of this Greek attitude can be seen in the work of the great twentieth century restorer of Greek thought, Leo Strauss, who insisted that the Greek thinkers had a doctrine of natural right, not a doctrine of natural law.[1]

Natural law thinking arose when "the Greek logos – metaphysics – was appropriated by the biblical theology of a creating and lawgiving God" (xix). In that original natural law thinking the divine law-giver was central. This version of natural law stands in need of "rediscovery," not only because natural law of any sort plays a lesser role in modern moral discourse than it once did, but perhaps more significantly, when it does play a role it does so in a drastically modified – Hittinger might say, distorted – form. He quotes the twentieth century legal philosopher H. L. A. Hart identifying "the continued reassertion of some form of Natural Law doctrine" as "due in part to the fact that its appeal is independent of both divine and human authority" (xii). The declaration of independence from authority, divine and human, began with the Enlightenment philosophers, according to whom "natural law came to mean the position of the human mind just insofar as it is left to itself, prior to authority and law" (xii). The cause of this embrace of "the opposite" of the traditional view was "the theologico-political problem" (xxv, 13, 14). Hittinger does not explain what he has in mind by "the theologico-political problem," but I take him to mean the set of problems initiated by the Reformation, as a result of which not only intense theological-theoretical conflicts arose, but serious political, even violent conflicts broke

---

1   L. Strauss, *Natural Right and History* (Chicago & London: The University of Chicago Press, 1953), 120–164.

out over the human ordering that should accord with the divine ordering(s) affirmed in the various theologies of the day. Thus Catholics not only fought Protestants (as in France) but different kinds of Protestants fought each other as well (as in England or Holland).[2]

My own researches agree to a large degree with this part of Hittinger's story – though I think it was a bit more complex than he gives it. The second great hey-day of natural law theories in politics occurred in the seventeenth and eighteenth centuries in the wake of the religious wars. Especially significant and conformable to Hittinger's narrative is the rise of Grotian natural law theory to prominence all over Europe in the seventeenth century. Grotius is famous or notorious for his "etiamsi" – even if God did not exist, the natural law he describes would exist.[3] This affirmation is clearly an attempt by Grotius to find universal and binding norms for moral and political life independent of the various contending partisan theologico-political commitments of the parties to the wars. The story is more complicated than Hittinger tells it, however, for many Enlightenment thinkers rejected the Grotian solution, and most especially his effort to find a natural law independent of God. Locke, for example, directly countered Grotius on that very point. Nonetheless, I do not mean to follow out this part of Hittinger's story, for on the whole it is accurate enough.

The Enlightenment thinkers, he maintains, used natural law to establish "an authority-free zone" (xi, xv, xvii, xxv, xxxvii, 14, 31–32). They were not, for all that, relativists – the point of natural law was still to find natural norms. But the long-run effect was much more pernicious. By 1992, the U.S. Supreme Court had pronounced its (in)famous decision in the case of *Planned Parenthood v. Casey*, a case that took the notion of an "authority-free zone" to its extreme (il)logical conclusion. Natural law has become a way to "subvert [...] an order of obligation prior to the positive law." The natural law (or some vaguely recognizable descendant of it) became a way of affirming the individual to be "a law unto himself," or more precisely, "the absence of legislative power is established by the right of the individual to be self-norming" (xxxii, 22–24, 36, 37, 47, 50). *Casey* represents the introduction of a new "paideia" (formative education) into the American regime: "the honoring of unbounded individual liberty" (200).

This broader story is relevant for understanding Hittinger's project of a "rediscovery" of Christian natural law in a post-Christian era, for it is the crisis of modern natural law that makes the project of recovery so urgent. As I need not tell those who have read the book, it is filled with astute analyses, pungent criticisms of modern doctrines, marvelous expositions of Thomistic natural law theory, and much wisdom both theoretical and practical. Despite that, I wish to

---

2   See my *Natural Rights and the New Republicanism* (Princeton, N.J.: Princeton University Press, 1994), Pt. I.

3   See *Natural Rights and New Republicanism*, Pt. II.

take issue with his implicit claim that his rediscovered natural law is the answer to our present ills. Had I more time I would even question his analysis of *Casey* and the nature of our contemporary crisis.[4]

The First Grace argues strongly for the position that natural law without God will not do. It presents two main lines of argument to arrive at that conclusion. In the first place, the Catholic tradition, all the way back to the Church fathers, has understood natural law as part of theology, i.e., as dependent on God. It was only with the aforementioned Enlightenment natural lawyers that the natural law drifted away (or was cut loose from) its theological grounding. Secondly, and even more insistently, Hittinger argues that without God the natural law cannot be a genuine law. It can only be a metaphorical law, an analogical law, or no law at all. Thus he resists mightily (as he did in his earlier book, *A Critique of the New Natural Law Theory*)[5] the view held by "some contemporary theologians [...] that natural law denotes the human practical reason." If one sees it that way, "its specifically legal character [...] is muted, if not abandoned" (46).

On the contrary, Hittinger maintains, natural law is properly law. He is not entirely clear on what turns on so holding it, but the main thing seems to be the affirmation that human beings always find themselves under a law, that is, having been given to them a guide to conduct that is obligatory and to which they are responsible (xv). As he says, "moral norms are laws" (50). He hardly mentions the issue of sanctions, but no doubt that is lurking somewhere.[6]

Hittinger provides very little by way of an independent argument for his theses about the lawful character of natural law. In most of the key places in his exposition he has recourse to Thomas Aquinas's presentation. Since much of the contemporary debate about natural law turns into a debate about Thomistic doctrine, this procedure is perhaps not too surprising. (However, one should compare his somewhat contrasting procedure in *A Critique*, 8–9). Accordingly, Hittinger cites Thomas' "well known [...] definition of law."

> Law is a binding ordinance of reason for the public good, actually promulgated by a competent authority. Thus, there are four principles: [1] ordinance of reason rather than force, [material cause], [2] for the common good, [final cause], [3] made by a competent authority [efficient cause], and [4] promulgated [formal cause]; each is a necessary but not a sufficient

---

4   On the latter, see my forthcoming "Casey at the Bat: Taking Another Swing at *Planned Parenthood v. Casey,*", in C. Wolfe, ed., *That Eminent Tribunal* (Princeton N.J.: Princeton University Press, 2004), forthcoming.

5   R. Hittinger, *A Critique of the New Natural Law Theory* (Notre Dame: University of Notre Dame Press, 1987).

6   See 53: "Of course, in the order of being, it is true that there is a legislative command backed by sanctions."

condition for something to be a law." (95)

If natural law is genuinely law, then it must have all four of these law-making qualities, (which correspond to Aristotle's four causes), including the third, a competent authority as efficient cause. Aquinas goes to lengths to demonstrate that the natural law has all four causes, and therefore is a genuine law. The "competent authority" who is the efficient cause of the natural law is God, as Hittinger points out when he repeatedly insists that Aquinas treats the natural law as a mode of the eternal law, which is, in turn, the law by which God governs the whole. Natural law is not a different law from the eternal law (as many interpreters of Aquinas seem to believe) (see esp. 8–12) but the special way in which human beings, the rational creatures, participate in the eternal law (8, 9, 16, 39, 44, 50).

As a genuine law, however, the natural law must also possess the formal cause of law, promulgation. As a rule for the action of rational beings the law must be available, that is, known or knowable, by those who are to use it to regulate their conduct. Although Hittinger is clear and unambiguous in his treatment of the efficient cause of the law, he is wavering and ambivalent in his (much less thematic) treatment of the formal cause, promulgation.

His most extended consideration occurs in the context of a critique of Francisco Suarez's treatment of the promulgation issue. As Hittinger puts it, Suarez, "of all the modern scholastic theologians [...] was perhaps the most alert to the problem of the legality of natural law" (51). This means for Suarez that "the obligatory norm [must] be known in reference to its point of legislative origin" (51). The norms and the source of the norms must both be known (promulgated) for natural law to qualify as genuine law. Suarez concluded there must be a "sign that bespeaks a divine lawgiver [...] in the concept of a moral precept" (52). Suarez holds that "the naturally known moral norms also – and in some sense simultaneously – require knowledge of the deed of the legislator in order to be grasped as norms of conduct" (52). One must know the norm, as, say, Aristotle mostly did, but one must also know that the norm has its source in the legislative act of God, and therefore one must know of a legislating God, as Aristotle did not. Suarez, as Hittinger reads him,

> held that there are two conditions for natural law being "law": (1) in the order of being, a God who legislates by instilling knowledge of the moral measures of action; (2) in the order of knowledge, a recognition that God so legislates and binds the creature to act according to his will (53).

Although Suarez claims to be in agreement with Aquinas, Hittinger insists he is not. "Suarez did not accurately represent the tradition 'held by St. Thomas and common to the theologians'" (55). Hittinger takes issue with Suarez by maintaining the distinction between the order of being and the order of knowledge. Where Suarez runs them together, Hittinger's Aquinas kept them apart. The legislating God is necessary in the order of being, but not in the order of knowledge. "When St. Thomas said that proper authority and promulgation are two essential traits of law, he did not stipulate that the recipient of the law necessarily has to know the legislative point of origin" (53). Aquinas "emphasizes the *legislated deed* regardless of what the recipient of the law knows about the legislative point of origin. Hence natural law is real law because basic moral norms are actually made-to-be-known (promulgated) to the rational creature who grasps the divine law 'naturally' (*naturaliter*)" (52). To support his reading of the Thomist position he rightly cites the following passage: "The natural law is promulgated by the very fact that God instilled (*inseruit*) it into man's mind so as to be known by him naturally" (*ST*, I-II, q. 90, a. 4 ad obj 1).

Thus as Hittinger reconstructs the Thomistic position, knowledge of the content of the natural law is (and must be) promulgated, but not knowledge of the lawgiver, or the source of the natural norms in God. "The *quid* of which they are conscious is moral good and evil, not necessarily the legislator" (54). This reading, Hittinger asserts, is also in accord with Paul's famous claim about the Gentiles' knowledge of natural law in *Rom.* 2:14 (54).

Hittinger believes the view he attributes is not only the authentic Thomist view, but it is also the philosophically superior view. Aquinas and the older tradition "distinguished more sharply than did Suarez between what is first in the order of cognition and what is first in the order of being;"; the natural law "is much weakened when it is forced to defend the intelligibility of natural 'law' on the basis of immediate cognitive evidence of the lawgiver." Suarez "transposed the terms of the older tradition in a way that made it less credible." He also "appears to make the natural law look like a positive law" (57). Unfortunately, Hittinger never gives a very clear account of these particular shortcomings of the Suarezean position. That it makes the natural law look more like positive law is the easiest part to understand and relates as well to Suarez's well-known attempts to bring together Thomistic rationalism and Ockhamist voluntarism. The Suarezean natural law, so far as it traces back so directly to the act of will of the divine legislator looks much less like a law immanent in the order of nature *per se*, and therefore looks more positive and less natural.

But the more significant of Hittinger's objections is the other. The chief problem seems to be that Suarez puts a demand on the natural law that it cannot satisfy, the demand that the divine legislator and his act of legislation be as evident ("immediately" available in "the order of knowledge") as the precepts of the law itself (51). This demand, which Hittinger considers unfulfillable, opens the way for the Enlightenment thinkers, who attempt to pursue natural law by collapsing the important distinction between the order of being and the order of knowledge. Hittinger's account of Aquinas on these matters is quite puzzling, however. As we have seen, he insists that Suarez is mistaken to think that

Aquinas believes the recipient of the natural law necessarily knows or even needs to know the divine legislator. "The promulgation" can be "effective even if the creature has only the foggiest idea of law's origin in the divine mind" (52). Yet, on the other hand, and in a more Suarezean vein, Hittinger also affirms the following: "St. Thomas thinks that a human agent ought to know, not just by argument, but by simple inference, that moral norms bind by virtue of something other than our own mind. [...] The movement of the mind from the effect (moral truth) to the cause (God) is something that in principle falls to the human reason" (54). Indeed, Hittinger quotes Aquinas to the effect that a person lacking this knowledge of God (as the cause and therefore legislator of the moral law?) is "very blameworthy" (293 nn. 49, 50). Of this inference, Hittinger says in a statement of masterly precision, "Thomas does not insist that it depends in principle on religious faith" (xx). Of course, if he did so insist it is not clear we would be justified in speaking of natural law any longer. But it is noteworthy that Hittinger does not make the more straightforward affirmation: that this inference does not depend on religious faith. Hittinger concludes this part of his discussion with the revealing claim that "Thomas shows no interest in making this inference depend on a formal demonstration. [...] He never argued that knowledge of a superior cause is exclusively the work of demonstration" (xxi). All of this is interestingly ambiguous. The upshot seems to be that many people, for non-philosophic or non-rational reasons, infer from the moral order a higher cause ("philosophically untutored inferences from the things that are, from tradition, and also, for Christians, from infused faith") (xxi).

It is not easy to put together all the pieces Hittinger serves up here, for they seem to ill cohere and at times contradict each other. His main point, not so baldly stated as this, however, seems to be that Aquinas does not take the Suarezean line because in point of fact a rational "proof" (demonstration) of the legislating divinity does not follow from the facts of moral consciousness. Perhaps the situation is this: the Thomistic-Hittingerean view is that God's existence (as legislative actor?) is inferable (demonstrable) in other ways and from other data, but not from moral data *per se*, but that many do (irrationally?) infer all that from moral data anyway. That position would distinguish Aquinas from Suarez, who affirms evidence of the divine legislator in the moral data themselves.

Yet Hittinger and Aquinas consider it morally blameworthy if the inference to the divine legislator is not made. To the degree that is true, they would appear to be drawing back toward the Suarezean position. The more considered Thomistic-Hittinger doctrine seems to be, however, that promulgation of the natural law does not require promulgation of the law-giver (in the order of knowledge), but merely the existence of the law-giver (in the order of being).

But Hittinger gives us remarkably little aid in understanding Aquinas's actual view about promulgation. Aquinas, we have seen, claims that the natural law is promulgated through being "instilled" in the human mind. This claim sounds much like the claim about innate ideas that Locke made such hash of in Book I of his *Essay Concerning Human Understanding*. One cannot help but suspect that Aquinas had something more subtle in mind than the relatively crude position Locke refuted.

Hittinger does not push this question very hard, but he concedes that the character of natural law as law depends on a satisfactory account of the law's promulgation, so let me briefly try my hand at it. In one of the two articles devoted to promulgation in the Question on natural law (*ST*, I-II, q. 94, a. 2, 4), Aquinas raises the question of "whether the Natural Law Contains Several Precepts, or One Only?" (a. 2). As he develops his answer, it becomes clear that the question of the substantive content of the natural law is inseparable from the question of its promulgation: what is known is inseparable from how it is known. The "precepts" of the natural law are several, and include the "first principle of the practical reason" (pace, Hittinger). Just as "being" is that which is self-evidently apprehended by the speculative reason, so "good" is the first principle self-evidently apprehended by the practical reason. The practical reason grasps "good as that which all things seek after," or, as a proposition properly of the practical (acting) reason: "good is to be done [...] and evil is to be avoided." Although there are other precepts of the natural law, this first principle of the practical reason has a certain privileged status, for "all other precepts of the natural law are based on this, so that whatever the practical reason naturally apprehends as man's good (or evil) belongs to the precepts of the natural law as something to be done or avoided" (a. 2 c).

The other precepts of the natural law are given by the natural inclinations, of which Aquinas gives us a brief but sophisticated account in the immediate sequel. The inclinations point to natural human goods. They are, in that sense, teleological, and remind, for example, of ancient philosophic accounts of human good. What is less than clear to this point, however, is why Aquinas says "all other precepts of the natural law are based on" the first precept. The answer seems to lie both in the particular relationship between the first and other precepts, and in the form of the first precept, notably different from the natural inclinations themselves. The latter point is particularly significant, for in form the first precept is a command: seek the good, avoid the evil. This is admittedly empty in itself, but the natural inclinations identify what the goods (and evils) are. The first precept thus enters into each of the others by transforming it from a proposition of the form "x is a naturally known good" into the form "seek (do) x." The first precept is the element that promulgates the natural goods in the form of commands, or, to put it otherwise, as laws. The combination of the first precept and the others (all naturally known and in a sense, but not a crude sense, infused) allows Aquinas to conclude that the natural law is sufficiently promulgated to qualify as a law, despite that fact that knowledge of God the legislator is not (as Hittinger says) also promulgated in this way.

If this, or some other account, captures Aquinas's views on promulgation, we can readily see Hittinger's point that Suarez has departed from the original Thomist position. This construct leaves Hittinger in an awkward position, however. If it is correct that the legal character of the natural law can in fact be adequately established by this argument, then the central claim he wishes to make in this book does not follow: it is simply not the case that there is no natural law without God, for Aquinas has arguably established the legal character without God. Now at this point, Hittinger will no doubt appeal to the distinction between the order of being and the order of knowledge. Aquinas knows that God is the legislator and the natural law is the mode of human participation in the eternal law. But many (most?) can know they are legally bound by natural law who do not know of its source in God. Their knowledge of the law and their obligation to it is apparently more evident than their knowledge of the legislator.

I believe it is not sufficient to appeal to the distinction between the order of being and the order of knowledge as Hittinger (and perhaps Aquinas) wish to do at this junction. This, I believe, is the point of Suarez's revision of inherited Thomist doctrine. The natural law is not a law like the law of gravity; it is law addressed to rational beings and appeals to their capacity for rational and voluntary action. The natural law binds them not because they can do no other, but because they understand the normativity and obligatoriness of it as a law. But Aquinas had insisted that the legality of law depended on the existence of a lawgiver. Here the distinction between the order of being and the order of knowledge must collapse: the natural law cannot be a law for those addressed by it unless all the elements that make it a law are promulgated, i.e., present in the order of knowledge. Either the general definition of law must be adjusted so that the legislator is not universally necessary to impart legal status to norms, i.e., to capture the adequacy of the argument about promulgation prescribed above, or one must accept the Suarezean emendation of the Thomist position, or one must concede that the case for natural law has not been successfully made. What one cannot do is stand where Hittinger does. There, Michael Jordan, is my jump shot!

A Response to Commentators

Russell Hittinger

As Tom Hibbs pointed out in his review of *The First Grace*, my collection of essays leaves the reader with "a sense that an important investigation is just getting started when it ends." My commentators here also point out that certain lines of thought are, at the very least, inadequately developed. While their observations and criticisms deserve serious response, I hope they will not begrudge the observation that *The First Grace* is not a systematic treatise on natural law. Rather, it is a collection of essays on one aspect – theoretical and applied – of natural law: namely, the *legality* of natural law and its implications for *human authority*.

It might be useful to remark upon the polemical context of many of the essays in this volume.

Most of the essays were generated by the Supreme Court's decision *Planned Parenthood v. Casey* (1992) and Pope John Paul II's encyclical *Veritatis splendor* (1993). What interested me was not so much their positions on abortion, but how they respectively situate human liberty in an order of law. Both make appeal to principles beyond the positive law. Both reconnoiter and stake out the jurisdictional boundaries of human authority, distinguishing matters which genuinely fall to the prudence of public authority and those which do not. Of course, *Casey* and *Veritatis* are not symmetrical in this regard, for the plurality opinion in *Casey* was satisfied to discover what, in the very nature of things, belongs to the decision of the individual. Having discovered this principle, the opinion could assert what cannot belong to the jurisprudence of the state. The constitutional rules and measures of jurisdictional authority were the conclusion rather than the starting point of the plurality opinion in *Casey*. In this sense, the opinion rests upon an argument from natural right. In *Veritatis*, on the other hand, the Pope is interested in something more than the question of what belongs, respectively, to the individual or to the state. Especially in the first two sections of the encyclical, the Pope investigates what, in the very nature of things, does not and cannot belong to the prudence of an individual. Not just what is prior to, and what shapes, the human law; but also what is prior to and shapes human liberty. Yet in both documents, natural law is invoked (albeit, covertly in *Casey*) to situate human practical reason along the border-line of freedom and authority.

The reader of *First Grace* is forewarned that this is the problem that gave rise to these essays. The problem is perhaps best summarized, or exemplified, in Chapter Four. What does the natural law have to say about authority to render judgment? This question, of course, cannot be kept wholly separate from what the natural law might have to say about the moral measures of particular acts, nor from the wider issues of public policy about such things as abortion, euthanasia, and so forth. At the same time, it is a distinct issue – one that is often avoided in contemporary discourse about natural law, despite the fact that it is the very thing under debate. To get it out into the open is useful not only for understanding disputed issues of our own time, but also for connecting our discourse about natural law to the work of past generations. Enlightenment thinkers such as Hobbes, Locke, and Rousseau were acutely aware that to speak of natural law was to consider the origin and location of authority. One month before the Declaration of Independence, Samuel West preached a sermon before the Massachusetts legislature. Entitled "On the Right to Rebel Against Governours," the sermon advances the proposition that "a state of nature is properly a state of law and government." Revolution does not necessarily throw the colonists into the condition of being under no authority, for even the so-called state of nature has a public law. Moreover, that law is higher than that of Parliament, and one to which men have an antecedent obligation to obey. Undoubtedly, 17th and 18th century philosophers, jurisprudents, and polemicists could and did have different opinions on whether there is a public law prior to that of human government. The point I want to make is that they understood that the question should not be suppressed, and that, from one point of view, it is the crux of the issue of natural law. Is natural law a "law," and if so, in what sense? Does appeal to natural law throw us outside the sphere of the rule of law? Do such appeals amount to a disobedient preference for mere private opinion, for biblical or secularist mythologies about the origin and location of human authority? Today, natural law is usually a theory of ethics that competes with other normative theories. But we should attend to natural law as a theory and debate about authority, if for no other reason than the fact that the 18th century problems are still with us. At least they were for me during the summers of 1992 and 1993 when I read and pondered *Casey* and *Veritatis*.

As these essays in *The First Grace* indicate, I was also intrigued by how much St. Thomas has to say about the deeper jurisdictional issues of natural law. These discussions are distributed rather far and wide in his works. One runs the risk of giving an imbalanced interpretation to comments he makes in connection with diverse subjects in so many different texts. By the same token, this diversity of problems and texts can also convince the reader that quite a lot depends, for Thomas, upon the legality of natural law.

Take, for example, the problem of whether an erring conscience can bind an individual. The question crops up in more than one of Thomas's works, but the discussion of it in *De Veritate*, question 17, articles 3-4, is his most complete treatment. Thomas contends that an erring conscience subjectively binds insofar as the individual "considers it the law of God" – that is, insofar as the individual considers himself under a higher law. "Although man is not higher than himself," Thomas reasons, "the one whose precept he knows is higher than man; this is how he is bound by his conscience." Also, take Thomas's vigorous objection to the Cistercian and Franciscan position that the second table of the Decalogue is dispensable if God so orders. The main issue was whether God commanded the patriarchs to violate the natural law by virtue of ordering Abraham to sacrifice Isaac or by permitting Abraham to take a concubine. The older tradition had argued that although God cannot dispense with the first table, for he cannot order men to another God, the second table, including the natural law precepts contained therein, are dispensable by divine fiat. Thomas held that every precept of the second table is an implication of duties under the first table. The commandment not to kill, for example, forbids men to usurp God's immediate jurisdiction over life and death. What we might regard as a purely moral issue of harm to neighbor is treated by Thomas as a jurisdictional issue. In his *Conferences on the Ten Precepts*, which were given about a year before his death, Thomas makes the jurisdictional issue even more prominent. I could not help but notice that this little-known work of Thomas was quoted and cited in *Veritatis splendor*.

I will not try to make a complete list of the disputed issues in which Thomas discusses natural law in terms of the broader question of legality and authority. We find it in his treatment of who has authority to make decisions about vows of marriage and virginity, in his treatment of how legislators and judges are differently situated to make judgments on the basis of natural justice, on the obligations of private and public persons to obey or merely comply or to outright disobey flawed commands of legal authorities, even on the question of Christ's judicial powers possessed as a natural right by virtue of his humanity.

I thought that such considerations are helpful as we try to make sense of our current legal and theological environment in which natural-law kinds of arguments are made to dissever morality and liberty from authority, and, more interestingly, natural law from the rule of law.

Response to Fr. Robert Gahl

I agree that it is necessary to say clearly that natural law in the human mind is really distinct from the eternal law. But when Thomas takes up this very issue, in *ST* I-II, questions 91 and 93, he uses the distinction between law in the mind of the legislator and law *in* the recipient of legislation. Natural law *as law* (and this is the matrix of the issue) is never *in* the human mind as it is *in* the mind of a legislator. In this sense (not in other senses), he contends that the eternal and natural laws are not diverse. One thing we never find ourselves doing is legislating natural law. What is properly in our mind is human law, for in this case we are not merely a secondary cause of promulgation but proximately the legislator. Here, we instantiate the active principle of law, using the natural law to make more legal rules and measures. I don't think, as Gahl suggests, that I exaggerate human dependency on a divine measure. I would be guilty of exaggeration if I denied that human beings were in any respect an active measure of law. Precisely because of our capacity to rationally receive the law we are capacitated to have an active share when we go on to make more law. Yet even in the case of human law, the human intellect is never a *measuring*-measure absolutely speaking. The human intellect, for Thomas, can never be said to be "law." We frame and impose laws by virtue of a higher measure.

So far as I understand it, this is why, in question 91 on the diversity of laws, Thomas finally adopts Augustine's position that there are only two: laws which proceed from the divine mind, and temporal laws which proceed from the human mind. This comports with his position that the proper definition of a law is drawn from the active principle, which is a mind actively conceiving, judging, promulgating. Since Thomas rules out angels as sources of legislation, there can only be two – divine and human. Incidentally, this is why Thomas has a very strong jurisprudential doctrine of "original intent."

I do take to heart Gahl's gentle but entirely accurate criticism that these essays leave woefully under-developed the pedagogy of the old law and the grace of the new law. The old law was the only concrete, historical legal system that Thomas ever treated in detail. Much of what he has to say not only about the natural law, but also the rule of law, is to be found in that discussion.

Of particular importance is Thomas's remarks in q. 100, articles 3, 5, and 11, on the two great love commandments, which, he insists, are *"per se nota* to human reason, either through nature or through faith." So foundational are these two commands, that all of the precepts of the Decalogue are referred to them as conclusions to general principles. Yet, in article 5, he proposes that it was necessary for men to receive a precept about loving God and neighbor because "in this respect the natural law had become obscured on account of sin." This raises the question of Thomas's assessment of the impairment even of the most rudimentary principles of natural law. While I agree with Gahl that Thomas's rubric "the time of natural law" is important, I am not prepared to grant it any normative importance. After all, in that same article, Thomas opines that this *tempus* is a punishment, meant to humble men.

Beyond fascinating issues raised by Thomas's treatment of the old law, I agree with Gahl that without consideration of the new law, my essays reduplicate the very sort of problem that I complain about: namely, leaving natural law isolated from theology. I should say, however, that Fr. Pinckaers' reaction against reducing moral theology to juridical concerns leads him to the other extreme of making law entirely secondary to virtue in moral theology. In his *Commentary on Romans*, Thomas writes: "But one cannot bring forward the testimony of some work which is good or evil, except through this: that he has an idea of the law."

Response to Joshua Hochschild

Let me begin by pointing out that at least two of the chapters do mount arguments, including moral arguments, drawn from natural law. Namely, the two chapters on judicial recourse to natural law. I am not sure I could make those arguments without premises derived from the legal character of natural law – premises, which, if they were scientifically justified, would be derived from natural theology.

I much appreciate Josh's thoughts on subsidiarity. As I understand it, subsidiarity is not a free-standing principle. Subsidiarity does not govern the distribution of roles and functions, or what the Roman documents since Pius XI call *munera*. Rather, subsidiarity presupposes that human beings already have and exercise certain roles: spouse, parent, priest, teacher, magistrate, and so forth. Subsidiarity does not tell us who has the roles, or proper roles. If subsidiarity is confused with the distribution of offices, roles, or functions, then we get the notion of *devolution*. (In England, for example, parliamentary power is said to devolve in favor of Scotland. This is only one small part of subsidiarity.) Subsidiarity commands that when help is given it must not absorb or destroy the *munera* of those being assisted. Thus, it has nothing to do essentially with issues of scale, that is, of smaller or greater. For example, in Catholic ecclesiology, there is a Petrine *munus* that is distinct from the ordinary episcopal *munus*. The issue is what *properly belongs* to a role, not the *scale*. Even though people usually speak of lowest possible level, this way of talking is not quite right.

In our time, the language of devolution and quantitative scale tend to strip away the older appreciation of the internal landscape of social forms, especially those which have a propriety, something their own, by virtue of nature and supernature. Of course, marriage bestrides the border of natural and supernatural social form, and we shouldn't be surprised that it is the lightning rod for our debates about whether the individual adopts social roles for merely functional purposes, or whether the roles have an ontological density that facilitates certain kinds of action and that makes claims upon the agent. Subsidiarity as it has been developed in Catholic social doctrine presupposes inherent social forms, and only secondarily powers. This is why Catholic liberals who appeal to subsidiarity for purposes of ecclesiastical decentralization are really appealing to devolution.

But this only brings us back to Hochschild's question of whether "certain forms of social association are in fact any more natural or proper than others."

I agree entirely that this is the main question. One could argue that the activities of a priest or a parent are inherently valuable – indeed, that they cannot be reduced either to scale or to cost-benefit analyses – and still assert that functions are interchangeable, for example with regard to gender. So, arguing for the inherent *value* of activities without also arguing for inherent social *forms* could produce a more egalitarian modular man.

Response to Matthew Levering

Dignitatis Humanae (hereafter *DH*) invites individuals and governments to recognize that the human person has a direct ordering to God; not just by virtue of supernatural life communicated by grace and sacraments, but also by virtue of the natural quest and duty to search out the truth about God. Precisely because of this twofold ordering, no human authority can claim competence to coerce acts of religious assent. One reason is that such coercion would deprive the assent of its proper act by depriving it of freedom. Interestingly, however, *DH* emphasizes the jurisdictional issue. Even the Church's authority to bind and loose are not peremptory with regard to the natural law or the law directly instituted by Christ. The twin legislative powers of the state and the church make, each in its own sphere, laws for persons who are already moved by God to ends. Of course, the motion supplied to a rational creature by nature and by grace are different both in kind and in dignity. But the source is the same. Just as the Church may not legislate contrary to the order of general providence, so too the state may not legislate contrary to the order of particular providence. Each power recognizes the dignity of man who is under a moral law (and for the baptized Christian, under a supernatural law) prior to the authority of human jurisprudence, whether civil or canonical. The freedom of the individual to pursue and submit to the truth about God, and the freedom of the Church to accomplish her mission, are rooted in divine providence.

Levering raises a problem of the first importance. Supposing that we can get beyond the caricatures of *DH* (that it endorses a right of conscience unmoored from natural and/or supernatural ordination; that it requires separation of church and state), Matt asks whether we can rely upon a non-confessional state to recognize the two rights delineated by the Council? Once upon a time, of course, the main problem was confessional states who claimed authority to govern the temporal life of the Church. As late as 1903, four European states still asserted the so-called *ius exclusivae*, that is, the right to veto a papal candidate. Indeed, that right was effectively used in the 1903 conclave by the Emperor of Austria, who delivered the veto via the Archbishop of Krakow. Although the President of France still enjoys a quasi-nomination right with regard to bishops in Alsace-Lorraine (the 1801 Concordat was not annulled by France in 1905, but it did not apply to these border lands with Germany), western secular democracies show no great appetite for directly governing the Church. France still has laws on the books regarding church property and monastic institutions, but they are usually not enforced severely. The federal system of Germany perhaps allows undue influence over church business by means of its tax supports, but this is largely the Church's own problem, for the Church willingly takes the money. The point remains, however, that so long as there is no deep and sustained conflict between Church and state, the secular democracies are inclined to stay clear of the institutional liberties of the Church, and one could say their track record for the past 50 years has been better than that of the 18th and 19th century states.

But I made the qualification: *so long as there is no deep conflict*. Such conflict is most apt to arise in connection with issues of abortion, euthanasia, marriage and divorce, private education, and employment – precisely in those areas where a *Casey*-like autonomy principle informs civil rights. Here, I would not be so confident that states will not try to make the church conform to a regime of morally lawless constitutional rights.

Moreover, American, Canadian, and European constitutional law have adopted ever more aggressively a new principle of religious neutrality, one which goes beyond an equal-protection stance – one requiring government at every level to take no cognizance of theological truths, whether those be of a philosophical nature or whether they derive immediately from divine revelation. In *Lemon v. Kurtzman* (1971), the Supreme Court forbade state legislatures from having detectable religious reasons or motivations for legislation that is otherwise completely secular. Here, then, we are not talking about a *de facto ignorance* of the appropriate grounds of religious liberty; rather, a *principled nescience*. The secular is not defined as the sphere of a temporal common good, but as a sphere in which knowledge of God must be absent. This does not comport with *DH*.

Interestingly, the bishops who drafted *DH* debated the issue of the nescient state. The penultimate draft of *DH* denied to the state any competence to make a theological judgment. That language was changed, for the good reason that such a far-reaching incompetence would undercut the state's obligation to recognize the ground of religious liberty, and thus undercut its ability to correctly ascertain its own limits in matters religious. In place of the sentence on incompetence, the final draft stated very simply that the state should not take over (in the sense of taking into custody, or usurping) the regulation of religious acts. Immediately after the Council, there was a raft of literature complaining the *DH* violates the principle of religious liberty by insisting that the reason for the right be public in nature. Since the *ratio* of the right includes reference to God, the Church introduces a principle of establishment under the cover of a right of liberty.

I believe we ought to clearly separate the problem of the nescient state from epistemological problems concerning knowledge about God. For the program of the nescient state does not rest upon facts about what people know or do not know about God, divine providence, the metaphysical ground of natural law, and so forth. Rather, the program rests upon what we are not allowed to introduce as knowledge for any public purpose. It sweeps into a single, undifferentiated category all propositions regarding You-Know-Who; and it matters not whether the propositions are derived from church creeds, philosophical reasoning, cultural traditions, or ordinary common sense untutored by speculative sciences. As Justice Stevens has recently asserted, even state recognition of religious liberty as an especially prized and protected good violates the principle of neutrality.

This program is indeed hostile to a higher law ground of rights. Nothing transcends human practical reason, except in private opinion. How, then, can such a program recognize and protect the rights spelled out in *DH*? In principle, it cannot. The ongoing effect of common sense and tradition may deter such a state from invading certain rights. But not for reasons depending on the right principle. What is most likely is that in liberal democracies devoted to the program of principled nescience, the state will defer to private judgment. Thus, in the case of abortion, individuals can choose for themselves whether to recognize an unborn child's right to life; in the case of marriage, the private parties can choose to regard marriage as a one-flesh unity of man and woman.

Whether there is a middle way between a confessional state and the nescient state is perhaps the main challenge posed to the post-WWII Catholic doctrine of the state.

Response to Michael Zuckert

Zuckert's queries and objections focus upon the issue of promulgation. I hope that my positions on this subject are not, as he suggests, incoherent or contradictory. I must say that if I were to come at these essays from a strictly philosophical standpoint, I would have selected just the chapter that Michael does, and I would have raised similar questions.

First, I take promulgation to be the efficient cause. The norm is actually communicated, made known. I am not inclined to understand promulgation as a formal cause because this is too close to post-Hobbesian positivism, according to which the fact of imposition of a law is the chief consideration of jurisprudence. For Thomas, the intellect is the formal cause of a law.

Since Thomas holds that God creates by efficiency, this allows him the notion of a promulgation by means of creation. For Thomas there are only two laws communicated in this fashion: natural law and the new law of grace, each of which, in analogous ways, cause a motion in the creature. In the case of natural law, by creating a nature; in the case of the new law, by creating a new *habilitas* in the soul.

The efficacy of natural law depends, in the first place, on the efficacy of creation. We can no more *not* know certain rudiments of natural law than we can

deliberately fail to exercise our natures. In this regard, Thomas does not attribute knowledge of the rudiments to innate ideas, but to natural inclinations to
form ideas on the basis of experience. The innate structure is not the concept so
much as the habit of *synderesis*. Whatever might be Thomas's "actual view
about promulgation," we can rule out innate ideas criticized by Locke. The efficacy depends, in the second place, on the rational creature's successful realization of the virtues and actions which perfect the rudiments. In the first place, we
cannot choose otherwise, and, so far forth, we are incapable of subverting the
communication. In the second place, in those things which need to be known by
the human intellect through acts of inquiry, reflection, and judgment, we are
capable of subverting the communication. Thomas is quite clear and insistent
that the primary precepts are known naturally, by exercising our nature; he is
also clear that intellectual and moral rectitude require something more than that.

Yes, in principle knowledge of the law-giver does not depend upon religious
faith. We might assume that Adam, in the state of integrity, did not enjoy religious faith in the biblical senses of the term. Nor did he enjoy the beatific
vision. Patristic and medieval theologians, however, maintained that Adam not
only understood the moral law but understood it precisely as moral law, that is,
in explicit relation to a law-giver. Otherwise, the test of obedience in Genesis
2:17 would make no sense. The exact nature of Adam's knowledge in this regard
was a subject of considerable debate among theologians. Franciscans held that
Adam was created in nature and then graced; Thomas held that Adam was
immediately created in nature and graced. All theologians attributed a grace to
Adam's knowledge, and all held that this grace was different than either the
grace of biblical faith or the miracle of direct infusion of God's essence via the
beatific vision. All supposed that Adam knew himself to be a creature in relation to God. He was given a knowledge of the lawgiver without need of the discipline of a science.

Thomas and Suarez do not differ on certain essential points. First, they
agree that natural law is real, indeed exemplary law. Second, they agree that the
rudiments of the natural law are efficaciously communicated. Third, they agree
that moral data are evidence of the lawgiver. In each of these ways, Zuckert
drives more of a wedge between Thomas and Suarez than what I had in mind.
Their difference consists, rather, in the fact that Suarez believed that the sign of
the lawgiver is immediately cognized without the labor of inference, and indeed
without the special graces given to Adam. He builds into the first apprehension
of the natural law a knowledge of the lawgiver, and this is bound to disappoint.
Among other things, it collapses the interesting problems and tensions posed by
the gap between moral data and the legislative source – it not only demotes the
formal and informal labors of natural theology, but it also glides over the role of
faith in remediating the problem discussed by St. Paul in Romans 1. Suarez
claims too much for the rudimentary knowledge of natural law; indeed, Zuckert

himself insists that a knowledge of moral obligation can be found in those who have little clarity about the lawgiver. That is exactly the point that I was trying to make. It is worth recalling that one of the first precepts of the natural law, according to Thomas, derives from the inclination to know the truth about God. This implies that there is something to be investigated; it does not, however, imply that the inclination is satisfied only in the mode of scientific proof.

I am not convinced that these two propositions are contradictory or incoherent: first, that knowledge of moral good and evil can be had without knowing the divine legislator; second, that having such knowledge of the legislator is very important.

It is possible to understand that one is bound by a norm without knowing the legislative pedigree. Imagine someone visiting a foreign country and seeing clearly enough that everyone drives on the left hand side of the road without knowing the legislative source of the norm. One does not subjectively feel un-obligated because of this ignorance. So, if the issue is whether the human intellect apprehends some aspects of moral obligation prior to an explicit or scientific understanding of how those norms are the effect of this or that legislator, I readily concede the point. By the same token, we should admit that there is something deficient if there is no knowledge of legislative pedigree. In the first place, there will usually be doubt about the public character of the norm; whatever we think of Hobbes, he can be credited for seeing the crippling effect of moral conviction without public authority; and I won't hesitate to agree that private moral conviction bereft of location in a scheme of authority is unsteady and brittle. When moral obligation bereft of public authority meets a system of moral obligation tethered in authority, it is predictable which one will win. Hobbes himself argues that the natural law favors the system of authority. But one needn't subscribe to a Hobbesian anthropology to make sense of this point. Thomas makes the same point in his discussion of the superiority of the old law, which re-established the rule of recognition about the law-giver and therefore the publicity of the moral law. And even more so in the new law, which capacitates and communicates to the creature the very spirit of the law, indeed of the lawgiver. So, to the question whether there is moral obligation without knowledge of lawgiver and the public measures of authority, the answer is yes. But whether this is an entirely natural condition, whether it is of the natural law, the answer is no. In my essays, I have tried to show why efforts to defend a natural law bereft of publicity and authority does more harm than good. This does not commit me to saying that no one can know that certain moral norms bind absolutely until they have erected the metaphysical and theological scaffolding that locates morality in the supra-public order. I do not think it is incoherent or contradictory to hold on the one hand that we can naturally know some moral norms even while being somewhat dislocated with respect to the legislative source, and, on holding on the other hand that this is not a very desirable condition.

What turns on the issue? First, whether human covenants are the origin of legally binding norms. Second, the brittle character of moral knowledge without the publicity of a rule of law. Even supposing some rudimentary knowledge of moral good and evil without knowledge of the lawgiver, the absence of publicity is usually devastating to society. Whatever one thinks of Hobbes' anthropology, on this part of the problem he was correct.

Finally, I don't think I can accept Zuckert's proposal that what is known is inseparable from how it is known. The natural law and the Decalogue, for instance, forbid murder, but the mode of promulgation is quite different. I believe that this is why Thomas refuses to diversify laws in 91 according to the modes of promulgation. A human law can be promulgated in writing, by word of mouth, or by custom. That does not amount to three different laws. In fact, diverse modes of promulgation need not imply three different systems of law.